Marry Wisely, Marry Well

A Blueprint for Personal Preparation

Ernie Baker

Shepherd Press
Wapwallopen, Pennsylvania

Marry Wisely, Marry Well
© 2016 by Ernie Baker

Published by Shepherd Press
P.O. Box 24
Wapwallopen, Pennsylvania 18660

Unless otherwise noted, all Scripture taken from the NEW AMERICAN STANDARD BIBLE®, Copyright © 1960,1962,1963,1968,1971,1972,1973,1975, 1977,1995 by The Lockman Foundation. Used by permission.

Typesetting by C and C
Cover Design by Tobias' Outerwear for Books

First Printing, 2016
Printed in the United States of America

B 22 21 20 19 18 17 16 16
11 10 9 8 7 6 5 4 3 2 1

Library of Congress Cataloging-in-Publication Data

ebooks: www.shepherdpress.com/ebooks

To Rebecca, Joshua, Jonathan, Joel, Elizabeth, and JoyAnna.
I am thankful to the Lord for the joy you have brought to my life and for the wise decisions you have made in your relationships.

Also, to the students of The Master's College.
Thank you as well for the joy you have brought to my life and I pray for you to make wise decisions in your relationships.

Contents

Foreword

I've mediated over six hundred divorces, most of which involved professing Christians. Nearly all of these marriages started with romance, confidence, and joy. But they eventually ran off the rails, bringing sadness, pain and regret to the couples, their children, and their extended families.

Marriage doesn't have to end this way, however. By God's grace, I've been happily married to the same marvelous woman for thirty years, and I love her more passionately (and wisely!) today than I did when we said "I do."

Nearly all of my relatives and close friends have enjoyed the same marital joy and stability. As a group, we defy the odds. Having weathered the early storms of marriage, we are gratefully experiencing a profound sense of oneness with our spouses as we move toward the finish line of life with our hearts knit tightly together.

If you'd like to enjoy this kind of lifelong, joy-filled marriage, I strongly commend this book to you.

Marry Wisely, Marry Well brings together wisdom principles from God's Word that can help you to develop the perspectives, character qualities and relational skills needed for a fulfilling marriage. First and foremost, these principles will help you see Jesus as the foundation and model for all of your relationships.

As you learn how to treasure and imitate Christ's love and wisdom, he will steadily conform you into his likeness, enabling you to grow in humility, empathy, gentleness and kindness. These character qualities will improve your ability to listen and communicate well, to offer timely encouragement, to confess your wrongs quickly, to offer genuine forgiveness, and to delight in serving your spouse.

I encourage you to read this book carefully and weave its wisdom principles steadily into your life, both today and for the rest of your life. This investment will produce relational dividends beyond your imagination, leading to a marriage that honors God, brings joy and fulfilment to your future family, and endures for a lifetime.

Ken Sande
Founder of Peacemaker Ministries and Relational Wisdom 360

Introduction

"What if I marry the wrong person?" "What if I wake up one day and realize that I don't love him any longer?" "What if she leaves me?" "What if he turns out to be a big weirdo?" "Will I ever get married?" Year after year, these are the types of fears I hear from college students. These fears were expressed most succinctly by a single man responding to a survey I gave to college students: "Finding the right person that you know you can grow old with and love forever, no matter what, just seems impossible."

Many have grown up in homes where their parents' marriage failed or where they knew their parents were not happy together. This, along with other cultural trends, has led to the current picture of marriage.[1] According to the National Marriage Project,

> As an adult stage in the life course, marriage is shrinking. Americans are living longer, marrying later, exiting marriage more quickly, and choosing to live together before marriage, after marriage, in-between marriages, and as an alternative to marriage. A small but growing percentage of American adults will never marry. As a consequence, marriage is surrounded by longer periods of partnered or unpartnered singlehood over the course of a lifetime.[2]

Let me state clearly why this book was written. I felt compelled to write first of all for my own family. The Lord has blessed Rose and me with six children (three boys and three girls). I love them dearly, and I am abundantly thankful to our Lord that five of them are married and their spouses are a blessing to them and us. We prayed for their spouses even before we knew who they were, but we also endeavored to help our kids think wisely about romantic relationships (yes, lots of talks). Even more important, we desired to help each one become a God-honoring person (even more talks). That is obviously the highest aim in life (1 Corinthians 10:31), but we also knew that if they were the right kind of person, they would more likely attract the right kind of person and be better prepared for marriage.

I am also compelled to write because I have the privilege of teaching wonderful students at The Master's College, and year after year I hear the same fears expressed about getting married. Even before coming to Master's, I was blessed to serve for almost fourteen years as a pastor near Virginia Tech University (Go Hokies!). Through the years, hundreds and hundreds of students passed through the doors of our church and our home. My wife and I spent many late nights discussing issues and concerns related to marriage. Even before that, I served on the staff of a church as the College and Career pastor. Marriage was often the topic in our Bible studies. College students are in my blood, and this book is for you.

Women and men can have romanticized notions of marriage. Young ladies dream about their Prince Charming who will rescue them and young men dream about a beautiful princess. Many marry with these views, believing they have found "true love" or "a soul mate," only to find their spouse is not what they thought. Somewhere along the line they get a reality check. They actually married another fallen human being who is not perfect. Her Prince Charming turns into a flaming dragon, and his princess transforms into the Wicked Witch of the West. The statistics concerning unsuccessful marriages in the United States are a sad testimony to this reality.

As the dreams of true love turn into a nightmare, those who observe it are left feeling insecure about the potential for their own success in marriage. The National Marriage Project has been doing extensive research concerning current attitudes about romance. They report that of 1,003 young adults surveyed, ages twenty to twenty-nine, "slightly more than half (52%) agree that one sees so few good or happy marriages that one questions it as a way of life." [3]

It ought to be obvious that we must be establishing romantic relationships in the wrong way. Of the many explanations for this outcome, a bottom-line answer is the biblical principle that you reap what you sow (Galatians 6:7). For example, many researchers are seeing the weakness of using cohabitation to find a spouse. They recognize that it misses many of the key ingredients for marriage, a chief one being commitment. Yet many couples still use cohabitation as the primary way to find a spouse.

Along with cohabitation, many other methods or combinations of methods are being promoted to find the right person. Visit a secular or Christian bookstore, and you will see shelves of books about relationships and the secrets of dating and mating successfully.

Maybe all of these options have led to confusion and you wonder, "What is God's way—dating, courtship, or a combination of both?" "Does your spouse just appear and you feel right about him?" "Does God speak to you in a voice and name the girl you are to marry?" Some think the answer is to just allow the parents to choose, and so they espouse a return to a betrothal approach. Each option has proponents claiming their way is best, wisest or most biblical. But Scripture gives us a wiser, more secure approach to finding the right someone.

This book is written to bring hope to those who are not married—in high school, college or beyond—a hope that you don't have to experience a failed marriage—hope that the Lord, through Scripture, will give you wisdom to choose a spouse. It is also written with the conviction that you can start preparing *now* for marriage—*before* you are in a relationship. Prepare yourself now by doing things that will lead to stability in your future home.

Usually, when I do premarital counseling, the couple is politely listening, though sometimes they are really tuned in. For the most part though, couples are just getting the required counseling over so that they can get to the most important thing—the wedding. Ideally I want to write to those who are not distracted by their emotions. I would like to get you to think about marriage while you can think clearly about your relationships without being distracted by an emotional attachment. I believe this will help you make a wiser choice. If you have never been married and are not currently serious about someone, or if you have already begun a relationship, this material is for you. Now is a perfect time to be thinking about how to make good choices in romantic relationships.

The emphasis in Scripture on making wise choices about everything in life would definitely apply to starting a family or as Scripture calls it, "building a house." Proverbs 24:3-4 is clear, "By wisdom a house is built, and by understanding it is established; and by knowledge the rooms are filled with all precious and pleasant riches." [4]

Even though the statistics given earlier relate to North America, the principles here will apply to believers on any continent since we believe that the Bible is timeless truth for all cultures. No matter how romantic relationships are formed in a country, biblical principles can still be used to give wise guidance.

I am writing not only as one who loves the Lord and his Word, but also as one who has been married for over thirty years. I love God's design for marriage and believe that God's way works.

So, let's leave the fantasy world of princesses and princes and get serious about building a future marriage house. You need to start building your house now, even before you know the person you will marry.

Let's start building!

Part One
Laying a Good Foundation

Part One explores foundational questions related to building a solid marriage house.

1. How is the term "house" used in Scripture? (Chapter 1)

2. What is your relationship with Jesus Christ and how does this relate to wisdom? (Chapter 2)

3. Why are we attracted to certain people? (Chapter 3)

4. What are God's purposes for marriage? (Chapter 4)

Chapter 1

BUILDING ON WISDOM

By wisdom a house is built, and by understanding it
is established; and by knowledge the rooms are filled
with all precious and pleasant riches.

Proverbs 24:3-4

I have many enjoyable memories of doing construction jobs with
my father. In fact, I helped build the house we lived in during part of
my teen years. I still think it's funny when I remember that snow fell
into it before we had the roof on, and I accidentally shoveled some
out a window onto a neighbor who was coming to meet us for the
first time. Thankfully, he was very forgiving. I also helped my father
construct the main building of a Christian camp. But, by far, the
most exciting project was remodeling a home that had an attic full
of snakes. I have a vivid memory of one poking its head out from
the side of the house, just inches from my face, as I was working on
a ladder. These projects were hard work, sometimes exciting and
always rewarding.

You Can Build a Secure House

As we consider how you can prepare for marriage, and especially
how to choose a spouse wisely, I know it will be a mixture of hard
work and reward as we see the principles of Scripture come alive.
It will also be exciting for you to see the changes the Lord wants to
bring about in you as you start to build now. The analogy of building

a house serves us well as we consider how to choose a spouse and prepare for marriage.

To demonstrate this, I'll explain how the term "house" is used in Scripture. Exodus 20:17 says, "You shall not covet your neighbor's house; you shall not covet your neighbor's wife or his male servant or his female servant or his ox or his donkey or anything that belongs to that neighbor." All of these together make up one's "house."

The concept of a family being called a "house" is also expressed in one of the most famous verses of Scripture where Joshua says, "As for me and my house we will serve the LORD" (Joshua 24:15). In the midst of surrounding idolatry, Joshua expresses enthusiastic commitment to the Lord. This reflects my own desire as I live in a culture that serves and is devoted to many things other than the Lord. I hope it is your desire also. But how is a house (family) like this built? How can you start now to build a home that has this commitment? These are the types of questions that will be answered throughout this book, but for now be encouraged that it really is possible. Even though it may seem impossible because of the failures and the misery we see, a wise home can be built. So, how do you start?

Reassurance from Scripture

Proverbs 24:3-4 gives us clear direction on how to build. These verses say, "By wisdom a house is built, and by understanding it is established; and by knowledge the rooms are filled with all precious and pleasant riches." Let's think more deeply about what this means.

"Establish" is a key word that means "to provide for or prepare."[5] It is used for preparing things from the beginning, at a basic level, or from the foundation up. Throughout the book of 1 Kings this word is used for "the ornate bases designed to support the ten brass lavers (basins) in the Solomonic temple."[6] It implies that, right from the beginning, something must be prepared properly so that it will be secure. According to this verse a house is established or made firm by "understanding," which is one of the many facets of wisdom. "Understanding" needs to be the firm foundation of your future house. Before going into more detail about what "understanding" involves, let's think about the role of the home's foundation.

The function of the foundation is to give the house a stable basis upon which the rest of the home is built. Wisdom is the foundation, the beginning of everything. When should you start laying this foundation of wisdom? Well, what would be the time to be wise? The answer is obvious—right now. Start learning the principles of wisdom now so that you can have a family in the future that glorifies the Lord. I believe you can start laying the proper foundation and even build the first floor of your future marriage home *before* you are in a relationship.

Let me give you some encouragement. This verse states that if a house is built by wisdom it can be established or made firm. The implications of this are very reassuring, especially since we are in a culture where marriage does not seem secure or, you come from a home where there has been divorce. You may even wonder, "Is divorce a curse that I cannot avoid if my parents were divorced?" Those of you who come from stable homes may also fear that your relationship will end in divorce since it is so prevalent in our culture. Be encouraged! Numbers 23:19 says, "God is not a man, that He should lie, nor a son of man, that He should repent; Has He said, and will He not do it? Or has He spoken, and will He not make it good"? You can have a well-established home. You don't have to be a divorce statistic. Be wise in the way you establish a relationship.

Reassurance from Research

Another reason to be encouraged is that research demonstrates that there are a lot of myths surrounding divorce. Studies indicate that a key to successful marriage relationships is the way they were established, and the things that were avoided (like cohabitation—even though culture might say this is wise). For example, Drs. Charles and Elizabeth Schmitz (in "Debunking the Divorce Rate Myth") state:

> Some researchers have reported that the highest risk factor for divorce is moving in together prior to marriage! Couples who do this have a far greater risk of divorce. In fact, couples who cohabit

before marriage —who give their "marriage" a trial run—have a divorce rate reported as high as 85%. Talk about the destruction of a myth!

We know that second and third marriages have high failure rates. Most studies report that second marriages have about a two out of three chance of failure—third marriages about a 75% chance. These second and third marriages, as well as those married four or more times, get lumped into divorce equations that are often reported. The simple truth is that the "impact rate" of divorce—those individuals that divorce *actually impacts*—is clearly much lower than the oft-reported rate of 50%. **Those married for the first time just need to learn to get it right the first time!** [Emphasis added]. [7]

So what are the factors that have major implications for the risk of divorce? Barbara Whitehead and David Popenoe in their book entitled *The State of Our Unions* (2004) reported the following:

1. *Couples with annual incomes over $50,000 (vs. under $25,000) have a reduced risk of divorce of 30%.* The message here is that couples contemplating marriage would be well advised to have income-producing jobs with stability before they get married.

2. *Couples who have a baby seven months or more after marriage (vs. before marriage) have a reduced risk of divorce of 24%.* The message here should be clear—bring children into the world when your marriage is ready.

3. *Couples who are 25 years of age (vs. under 18) have a 24% less risk of divorce.* The American divorce rate has been going down since 1981 because people in love are waiting longer to get married. Gaining education, experience, **and the wisdom that comes with age will certainly contribute to the success of a marriage** [emphasis added]. [8]

4. *Couples that consider themselves religious or spiritual (vs. not) are 14% less likely to get divorced.* Faith and spirituality contribute to the sense of oneness felt by successfully married couples. [9]

5. Couples who have some college (vs. high school dropout) have a 13% less chance of divorce. Education almost always leads to enlightenment and understanding, and more tolerance for the views of others. This is so critically important in successful marriages. In summary, reasonably well-educated couples with a decent income, who are religious or spiritual, who wait awhile to have children, who come from intact families, and who marry later in life (25 and beyond), have a greatly reduced chance of divorce. [10]

It ought to be clear—as you construct your family, wisdom helps guard against divorce. Also, secular researchers don't even talk about the impact the gospel makes on a couple's relationship (such as, learning to forgive just as we have been forgiven) or the stability that comes to a home by endeavoring, by God's grace, to live out biblical principles. You can have security in your marriage. If you sow as wisely as you can, you will probably reap a much more secure marriage than those who just follow the typical patterns of our culture.

Identifying Wisdom

Now that we have talked about the significance of laying the right foundation, let's get more specific about the components of the foundation. I remember mixing concrete to pour into the foundation of a home we were building. The mixture had to be just right for the concrete to be solid. I combined sand, the concrete mix with the correct amount of water, and then some gravel. All of this had to be blended well and poured into the forms, so that when it hardened, it became the foundation. We have already seen in Proverbs 24 that the foundation is "understanding." This is another word for wisdom in the book of Proverbs.

Wisdom has many dimensions; it is like a rainbow with its separate yet mixed colors. Maybe a better analogy would be a kaleidoscope with all its various shapes, hues and colors mixed together. As the kaleidoscope is turned, it creates different images that are just as beautiful as the last. Wisdom has a number of words and concepts to describe it, and all the various combinations are beautiful as they are put into practice in the wise person's life.

Wisdom Defined

Proverbs 2:6 gives a good definition of wisdom. "For the LORD gives wisdom; from His mouth comes knowledge and understanding." In the first phrase the word *wisdom* is used, but then two parallel words are used to further expand its meaning. [11] In fact, you could say that the combination of those two words, knowledge plus understanding, forms the definition of wisdom. Some of the other words in the book of Proverbs used to make up the rainbow of wisdom are prudence (1:4), discernment (2:3), and discretion (2:11). Here's how others have described biblical wisdom:

> Like all [Hebrew] intellectual virtues, wisdom … is intensely practical, not theoretical. Basically, wisdom is the art of being successful, of forming the correct plan to gain the desired results. Its seat is the heart, the centre of moral and intellectual decision (cf. 1 Kings 3:9, 12). [12]

> Biblical wisdom is both religious and practical. Stemming from the fear of the Lord (Job 28:28; Psalm 111:10; Proverbs 1:7; 9:10), it branches out to touch all of life, as the extended commentary on wisdom in Proverbs indicates. Wisdom takes insights gleaned from the knowledge of God's ways and applies them in the daily walk. [13]

Applying Wisdom to Marriage

Let's consider with detail and practicality what this means, especially as it applies to making a wise choice of who to marry. Since Proverbs 2:6 is giving us a definition of wisdom, then we could say it is the right knowledge of a subject plus understanding how to apply it. This Hebrew word for knowledge means to, "be acquainted," "knowledge gained in various ways by the senses," "contemplative perception" or, the "technical knowledge or ability such as that needed for building the tabernacle." [14] The word *understanding* has to do with discernment or making choices between options. [15] Having the right information is not enough. A lot of smart people may know a lot of information, but that does not guarantee they are wise. You have to know what to do with the information.

Applying this to building a future marriage relationship wisely would mean that you gather the correct information (knowledge) and then use discernment (understanding) to judge how that information applies to the potential relationship. Doesn't this have to do with knowing the right questions to ask to get the correct information? You not only need to know the right questions to ask of yourself (Why am I attracted to this person?), you also need to know the right questions to ask about a potential spouse (What is this person's commitment to the Lord?). This also implies that you need to learn the abilities and characteristics that make healthy relationships, and contemplate the things to avoid so that you don't have unhealthy relationships. You will find many of these questions throughout the book.

Figure 1 pictures this. We begin with a proper foundation and then build the first story, constructed of wise principles you can apply to yourself in your current relationship or as you prepare for a future relationship. If the other person is also following these same wise principles, you can have a solid second floor, which results in a relationship that glorifies the Lord.

Three Reminders

At this point I would like to emphasize that you must be cautious about three things. The first is that you will have to be careful of your *emotions and desires* as you start to think about romantic relationships. Emotions and desires have a forceful way of clouding your thinking. American culture tells you to "let your heart be your guide." As a result of having been guided solely by their emotions and sinful desires, many people have ended up with misery in their lives instead of enjoying the blessings of a God-glorifying marriage.

"By wisdom a house is built and by understanding it is established; and by knowledge the rooms are filled with all precious and pleasant riches."

-Proverbs 24:3-4

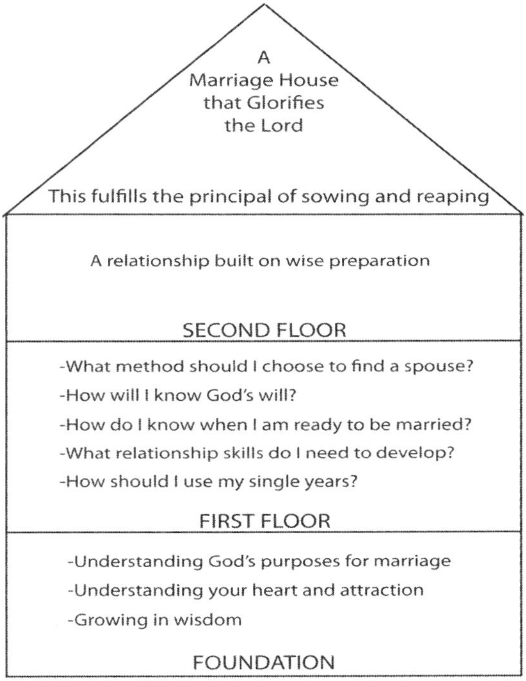

A
Marriage House
that Glorifies
the Lord

This fulfills the principal of sowing and reaping

A relationship built on wise preparation

SECOND FLOOR

-What method should I choose to find a spouse?
-How will I know God's will?
-How do I know when I am ready to be married?
-What relationship skills do I need to develop?
-How should I use my single years?

FIRST FLOOR

-Understanding God's purposes for marriage
-Understanding your heart and attraction
-Growing in wisdom

FOUNDATION

Figure 1

Second, there is something wrong with the conventional ***wisdom of the world***—it should be rejected. Our society tells you to live together with a potential spouse and that sex before marriage is the norm. The world also tells you, "traditional marriage does not matter any longer, it's old-fashioned and doesn't work." You can tell true wisdom by the fruit it bears, and a lot of bad fruit is coming from that "wisdom!" According to James 3:13-17, "Who among you is wise and understanding? Let him show by his good behavior his deeds in the gentleness of wisdom. But if you have bitter jealousy and selfish ambition in your heart, do not be arrogant and lie against the truth.... But the wisdom from above is first pure, then peaceable, gentle, reasonable, full of mercy and good fruits, unwavering, without hypocrisy."

Finally, another well-known verse challenges us to consider that, "Unless the Lord builds the house, they labor in vain who build it" (Psalm 127:1). Individuals who are ***not committed to God's ways*** but are more concerned about getting what they want rather than what

God wants in a relationship will labor in vain. Commit to God that you want him to build your house. As we will see in the next chapter, God's Word promises that when you allow him to build your house, it will be built upon the solid Rock.

It is one of the themes of this book that the way society is currently building relationships is not working because they are starting the construction unwisely and too late. I would urge you to commit to starting the construction of your future marriage house even before being in a relationship. If you are already in a relationship, then begin to evaluate it according to the principles you find in this book. It may be hard work, but you will make exciting discoveries along the way, and I know you will agree that it's rewarding (especially as you become the right person and then find the right person). As Scripture says, "You reap what you sow" (Galatians 6:7).

Starting to prepare now:

1. Define biblical wisdom and ask yourself if you are committed to it.

2. Write down what you found encouraging from this chapter and also what was challenging to you.

3. Try to identify what kind of fruit the "wisdom" of your life is bearing?

4. Write out a prayer of commitment telling the Lord that you desire your future "house" to be built wisely upon the principles of Scripture.

Questions to ask about a potential spouse:

Is this person also pursuing biblical wisdom and what evidence is there that this is true?

CHAPTER 2

CHRIST: THE FOUNDATION OF WISDOM

> Christ Himself, in whom are hidden all the treasures of wisdom and knowledge.
>
> Colossians 2: 2b-3

Let me tell you a story that is funny now but did not seem so at the time. One of the first homes my wife and I lived in had a poor foundation. It actually had hollow places where either the cement had not been filled in properly, or the dirt underneath had fallen away after the house was constructed. During the early hours of one morning, while we were asleep, a pungent odor jolted us both upright simultaneously, and I yelled, "What is that?" Unfortunately, we found out the hard way that skunks had made our weak foundation their home. They were eventually trapped and taken out into the woods where they belonged. Because of the poor foundation, the rest of the house was affected. There were cracks in the walls, and the floors were uneven. Looking back, I cannot understand why that house had not been condemned!

The Lord, the Secure Foundation

Even though the foundation rests below the surface, and normally can't be seen, it certainly affects everything. I'm sure you do not want a marriage home where the walls are developing cracks because of a poor foundation. Let's make sure to build a solid foundation.

As we saw in the last chapter it is obvious the proper foundation for a person's life is wisdom that is built upon the Lord. Proverbs 1:7 states, "The fear of the LORD is the beginning of knowledge …" (also Psalm 111:10). If you want a life based on the wisdom that Proverbs promotes, you must have a life based on knowing and understanding the Lord and believing that he is a God worthy of awe and respect. So then, let's get to know him.

It is easy to see in Scripture that the way this happens is in Jesus Christ. Paul writes that in him "are hidden all the treasures of wisdom and knowledge" (Colossians 2: 2-3). That's amazing. Our Savior himself is the embodiment of this wisdom, and by knowing him we have a direct connection to wisdom. In these verses Paul was answering the false teachers who had infiltrated the church and were teaching the people that they needed special, mystical knowledge; that what they had in Christ was not enough. These teachers believed that they had extra information the people needed. To argue against this, Paul writes in Colossians 2:10, "in Him you have been made complete." Paul was saying that you have all that you need in your Savior. So, your relationship with Christ is the main ingredient you need for wisdom in life. This ought to be deeply reassuring. Because you are complete in Christ, and in him are hidden the treasures of wisdom, you also have the rich resources you need for knowing how to choose a spouse and prepare wisely for marriage.

Matthew 7:24-27 states:

> "Therefore everyone who hears these words of Mine, and acts upon them, may be compared to a wise man, who built his house upon the rock. And the rain descended, and the floods came, and the winds blew, and burst against the house, and yet it did not fall, for it had been founded upon the rock. And everyone who hears these words of Mine and does not act upon them, will be like a foolish man, who built his house upon the sand. And the rain descended, and the floods came, and the winds blew and burst against that house, and it fell, and great was its fall."

These vital verses help describe the disasters many are experiencing in marriage today. Many marriages are falling apart under the storms of life, and many are strained as the storms of life beat against their house. They have failed to build their house with a foundation of wisdom found only in commitment to Christ.

Even though the following statement was written about education, the founders of Harvard University stated this same idea in 1636.

> Let every student be plainly instructed and earnestly pressed to consider well the main end of his life and studies is to know God and Jesus Christ which is eternal life (John 17:3) and therefore to lay Christ in the bottom as the only foundation of all sound knowledge and learning. And seeing the Lord only giveth wisdom, let everyone seriously set himself by prayer in secret to seek it of Him (Proverbs 2:3). [16]

This type of commitment to Christ, his ways and his wisdom, will guide you and protect you as you navigate the hazards in the rivers of life. It can guide you so that you do not end up smashing into the rocks by making a poor choice of a life partner. I do not know who said this (I wish I had) but it is so true, "Your relationship with Christ is the source from which all else flows."

Is Your Life Built on Christ?

How do you know if your life is being built on Jesus Christ? In the famous "Great Commission" our Lord tells us, "Go therefore and make disciples"(Matthew 28:19-20). He doesn't just say go tell the world a message about him, but go make followers of him. There's a big difference. As will become clear, I believe that the gospel is not just a message to believe, but is also a Person to follow.

Then what does it mean to be a follower of Christ? I believe it is the same as saying your life is built upon the foundation of Christ. If this is true, then how do you become a true follower of Christ or build your life on him? There are certain things you must believe, and this belief must be demonstrated in your life. Scripture teaches there is always fruit that shows true belief (see Acts 26:20; James 2:17). When this type of faith is operating in your life, he is the Master and you are the follower. Let's start from the beginning.

The Existence of a Sovereign God

God's Word starts with a basic assumption that there is a Creator of the universe to whom we are accountable. "In the beginning God created" is not only the opening phrase of the Bible but is also foundational to what we believe. In our increasingly secular cultures it is important to acknowledge the whole message of Scripture. Part of the central message is who the true and living God is, and how the world turns away from him and worships elsewhere.

This God is the One who determines right and wrong because he is the Creator. Because he made everything, he makes the rules about how everything functions best. This is not our world; we don't own it. We are living in his world. He is our environment. As Acts 17:28 says so succinctly, "In Him we live and move and exist...." Psalm 24 emphasizes that, "The earth is the LORD's, and all it contains, the world, and those who dwell in it. For He has founded it upon the seas and established it upon the waters." It is clear who is in charge!

As amazing as it is to realize we live in a world created by the one true God, it is even more amazing to accept that we were made to be in relationship with him. In Genesis 1:26-27 God says, "Let Us make man in Our image.... And God created man in His own image, in the image of God He created him; male and female He created them." As image bearers of God, we are made to be intimately related to him; therefore, it could be said of humans that we reflect his image. We are made to acknowledge him, talk to him, enjoy him and his creation, and even call him Father.

The Arrival of Sin

But something went radically wrong, and this relationship was broken. One of the earliest chapters in Scripture relates the sad story of how humans distrusted this amazing Creator God, decided to do things their own way and were justly punished because of this sin. We all have been living with a "Genesis 3 hangover" ever since. [17] It is clear in the opening chapters of Genesis that this condition is particularly evident in our relationships. God provided his Son as the remedy to this dreadful situation, to restore our relationship with our heavenly Father (John 14:6). One beautiful result of a restored relationship with him is a restored relationship with others.

To get the full impact of this dreadful situation we must understand what sin is and is not. What is your definition of sin? It's not a word that people use much anymore. First John 3:4 is one of the clearest verses for defining sin: "Everyone who practices sin also practices lawlessness; and sin is lawlessness." According to this verse it is sin to break God's laws. God is the Creator and King and as such he has the privilege of determining what is right and wrong in his kingdom. But we break his laws as naturally as we breathe, because we have a sin nature. As someone has wisely said, "We are not only sinners because we sin, but we sin because we are sinners." It is part of the essence of being human.

Sin is not just our lawlessness, but can also be defined as us seeking satisfaction elsewhere. Jeremiah 2:12-13 states, "'Be appalled, O heavens, at this; and shudder, be very desolate,' declares the LORD. 'For My people have committed two evils: they have forgotten Me, the fountain of living waters, to hew for themselves cisterns, broken cisterns, that can hold no water.'" We have a natural inclination to look to other things for refreshment for our souls, rather than to the Lord as our chief satisfaction.

Isaiah 55:2 clearly portrays this basic tendency of humans to seek satisfaction in things that don't really satisfy. "Why do you spend money for what is not bread, and your wages for what does not satisfy? Listen carefully to Me, and eat what is good, and delight yourself in abundance." The chapter then extends an invitation to turn from these things to the true and living God.

There are so many things in life in which we can seek fulfillment—intimacy, possessions, sports, and education. None of these are wrong if they are kept in their proper place as being done in submission to our Lord, viewed as good gifts from him and done as an act of worship to him. Our natural tendency, though, is to gravitate to these things first, thinking they are the essence of life. But, real meaning and purpose in life comes in relationship to the Creator (see Romans 1:25).

Since we are studying relationships it seems wise to use an illustration here about a person in Scripture who was seeking ultimate fulfillment in life in the wrong way. We commonly call her "the woman at the well" and her story is in John 4. Let's pick up this heart penetrating story with the Lord inviting her to drink "living water."

In verse 14 Jesus says to her, "Whoever drinks of the water that I shall give him shall never thirst; but the water that I shall give him shall become in him a well of water springing up to eternal life." She thinks he is referring to literal water, still not realizing who is talking to her. So, the Lord goes deeper and says, "Go call your husband." She answers very briefly, and maybe with shame, "I have no husband." He then says (and this is the reason I chose these verses for us to consider), "You have well said, 'I have no husband'; for you have had five husbands; and the one whom you now have is not your husband." She had to be shocked. Why did the Lord bring up the issue of all these men when he is offering her living water? How do the two connect? I believe the Lord was saying to her something like, "You think you need men to satisfy you. Don't you see how this desire is failing you? You've now had five husbands and are living with a sixth. Don't you see how these desires are leading you the wrong way? You think you need a man, but you really need me to be the water of your soul." The woman at the well represents the many who look to other things for deepest satisfaction, when Jesus was meant to be the One who brings meaning to life.

The Desperate Situation

We have already established that God is King, that we have violated his standards, and that we have a completely natural tendency to go to places other than him to find the deepest meaning in life. Let me ask you a question: when someone goes against a king's rule, what is it called? Treason. What then is the penalty for treason? "Off with his head!" is what a king might say. Does it make sense now why Scripture warns, "The wages of sin is death"? You may object and say that this God is cruel or that he is trying to ruin all of your fun, but remember, he knows how everything was designed to function, he knows that if the design is not followed it leads to destruction.

Scripture also makes it clear that if we have broken one of God's laws then we are guilty of breaking all. James 2:10 states, "For whoever keeps the whole law and yet stumbles in one point, he has become guilty of all." Lawbreakers are criminals. It is an ugly picture, but we are actually treasonous criminals because of the disloyalty and false worship of our hearts.

It should seem abundantly clear by now that we are in a dire situation. Doesn't this situation make the Savior look even more glorious? Romans 5:20 is a great encouragement, "But where sin increased, grace abounded all the more."

The Rescuing Savior

Like a knight riding in on a large white horse, our Savior came to rescue us from sin. First John 3 encourages me because it promises that he came to "destroy the works of the Devil." I need that encouragement in the fight against my sin nature. Not only that but he died on the cross to pay the penalty for your sin by taking your place. He gave his life to spare your life. He then rose again to demonstrate his victory over death and the Father's acceptance of that sacrifice (1 Corinthians 15:1-4).

According to John 1:12 you must believe this is true, but this belief is more than intellectual acknowledgement of facts. It is a belief that yields to him (see also John 3: 36). It is a faith in him instead of whatever you have been trusting in to get you through life. It is becoming a follower of Christ (one of his disciples). The woman at the well had given her life to be a follower of relationships. She turned from that to Christ. May I ask, to what have you given your life? What do you pursue?

Switching Loyalties

For years I have appreciated Paul's testimony in Philippians 3 even though I only viewed it as his personal testimony. Now I see it as a pattern for all true followers of Christ. Though your story of conversion will not be as dramatic, the pattern should be similar.

It is clear what he served in the past. Paul says, I am "of the nation of Israel, of the tribe of Benjamin, a Hebrew of the Hebrews … as to zeal a persecutor of the church ..." Just as the woman at the well was living to find the perfect man for fulfillment, Paul was living with Judaism as the center of his life. The woman at the well was serving relationships, and Paul was serving a religious system. The woman at the well's life revolved around men, Paul's around his pedigree, pursuit of education and other things. These things were the "lords" of their lives. The energy and devotion of their lives was dedicated to these things. As soon as we acknowledge our own false religious hopes, we see clearly that we need to turn away from them. What do you serve?

Turning From/Turning To

Each of them turned away from what they were pursuing, and considered them empty pursuits compared to following Christ. Paul says, "But whatever things were gain to me, those things I have counted as loss for the sake of Christ" (Philippians 3:7). He said this because there was Someone of greater value to pursue. He goes on, "I count all things to be loss in view of the surpassing value of knowing Christ Jesus my Lord." Do you see what he is saying? It is about his value system; what he then treasured and what he now treasures.

If you acknowledge these things, then you are accepting the message that Scripture calls the gospel. To accept this message is to yield your life to Christ and become a follower of him. The gospel is not just a message to believe; it is a person to follow.

It's time to ask some pointed questions. What is your testimony? What were you serving before becoming a follower of Christ? Are you committed to him as the central person in your life, or do you think that true security comes from a romantic relationship? I ask these questions with the deepest sincerity you can imagine, because your eternal relationship with Christ could be revealed by your answers.

These questions are also significant for the security of your future marriage. "Are you looking to marriage to make you happy or complete, to give you identity or purpose?" [18] Are you looking for something in relationships with others that only a relationship with Christ can deliver? This is easy to do with romantic relationships.

When this happens, Christ is no longer your Lord in a practical way. Marriage is a wonderful gift from God. Yet do you think getting married will provide meaning in your life? Direction? Security? Self-respect? Do you hope marriage will remove a sense of despair, inadequacy, failure, bitterness, or isolation? Do you say to yourself, "If only I could find a husband, then I'll be happy," or "I can finally find love, acceptance and security if I get married," or "My life is a failure unless I get married. [19]

When you have surrendered your life to Christ, you have begun a journey of knowing the One who is the embodiment of all wisdom and knowledge. He will teach you his wisdom for life in general, and in particular for choosing the right person to marry. When we become followers of the Lord, he becomes increasingly the center of our value system, and this helps protect us from idolizing relationships and making others the "rock" in our lives instead of the One who is the true Rock (see Psalm 18:1-3). I hope you will yield to him today.

Learning Christ's Wisdom

Now that we have addressed the question of what wisdom is and we've answered what it means to be a follower of Christ, we must now answer the question "How do you learn his wisdom?" To answer this, we need to go back to Proverbs 2.

To demonstrate how vital this is for answering the question of how to choose a spouse wisely, please read Proverbs 2 and notice what you are "delivered" from if you strive for wisdom (see verses 12 and 16).

Proverbs states that wisdom will "deliver" you from dangerous relationships. It will give you the discernment, all things considered, to know a good relationship from a poor one. I say all things considered because proverbs are meant to be interpreted as general maxims for life. In other words, generally speaking, this is how life works. For example, a young man is told that if he will pursue this kind of wisdom, God will give it to him, and a likely outcome is that he will choose to stay away from deceitful men (Proverbs 2:12).

It is obvious that wisdom is demonstrated by the choices we make. In Proverbs 1:10, Solomon warns his son to stay away from those who would lead him astray. This principle applies to romantic relationships as well.

Digging Diligently for Wisdom

How do we obtain this kind of wisdom? It's found through hard work just as digging for silver or gold is hard work. In Proverbs 2, this is the point of the "if-then" construction in the first five verses. If we are diligent to do what the first four verses say, then God does what the following verses state. Verse 6 says that God gives wisdom, and the first four verses tell us the type of person to whom he gives his wisdom. Why would the Lord make it hard to get? Let me give you three reasons why the Lord reserves this wisdom for those who are willing to work hard to get it:

1. The effort we expend shows the degree of our seriousness in wanting wisdom. If we really want something, we will work hard for it. This wisdom is a precious gift (Proverbs 3:13-15), and the Lord desires to give it away, but he wants to entrust it to those who are serious about the search. It's worth it!

2. Because of our sin nature, it takes diligent effort to acquire wisdom. By nature we are not wise (even though we think we are). Remember that Proverbs 22:15 says, "Foolishness is bound up in the heart of a child …" Part of this foolishness is laziness, so to get something as valuable as wisdom, we have to work hard to overcome our own nature and to humbly depend on the Lord. It's worth it!

3. The Lord is interested in using our struggle in seeking wisdom to teach us wisdom. We actually learn wisdom through the process of struggling to learn wisdom. The Lord is not only interested in the product of wisdom, but in the process of getting it. He wants us to change to be like the One who is the foundation of wisdom and the embodiment of wisdom—Jesus Christ. It's worth it!

Getting godly wisdom upon which to build a marriage house is worth any struggle or effort required. When we remind ourselves of the high rates of divorce and marital dissatisfaction, we should be motivated to diligently pursue wisdom. "How blessed is the man who finds wisdom, and the man who gains understanding. For its profit is better than the profit of silver, and its gain than fine gold. She is more precious than jewels; and nothing you desire compares with her" (Proverbs 3:13-15). It is as if God is promising, "In this mine of Scripture are nuggets of truth that you will find if you search for them, and if they are used, they can protect you from divorce and many other pitfalls in relationships." Now that's a reward worth searching for.

If this sounds like hard work, and you think that you may never be ready for marriage, let me assure you that the Lord promises, "My grace is sufficient for you, for power is perfected in weakness …" (2 Corinthians 12:9). Your job is to do the best that you can to live by his principles in a disciplined way. His responsibility is to work these principles into your life, and to give you the strength that you need (see Philippians 2:12, 13).

Diligently seeking wisdom is also worth it because it is so easy for your emotions and desires to go wild over that special someone, and then you stop thinking clearly. This is what happened to two young men I counseled. They both thought that their marriages would be secure because they were marrying a "Christian," but there were warning signs that they ignored because they were so "in love." Sadly, each was left by his wife. The pain that these young men have gone through would be hard to describe. Both of them now wish that they had pursued God's wisdom in choosing a marriage partner.

Digging With the Right Attitudes and Actions

To guard against unwise choices, you need to learn some principles of Scripture and apply them to your potential relationships. So, what is your attitude toward the wisdom of God's Word? The wisdom promised to us is directly related to the teachings of Scripture. This means that perhaps you need to adjust your attitude to that of the psalmist who wrote, "Your testimonies are wonderful; therefore my soul observes them. The unfolding of Your words gives light; it gives understanding to the simple. I opened my mouth wide and panted, for I longed for Your commandments" (Psalm 119:129-131).

Psalm 19:7 also makes this point, "The law of the LORD is perfect, restoring the soul; the testimony of the LORD is sure, making wise the simple." This verse promises to everyone who seeks wisdom that God's Word gives wisdom. This is essential when we are making one of life's most important decisions.

Your mindset should be that you truly want to receive God's Word. "Make your ear attentive to wisdom, Incline your heart to understanding" (Proverbs 2:2). To receive this wisdom you must have a teachable spirit, and should go to Scripture thirsty, asking the Lord to satisfy that thirst. Go to church with your ears open to hear the instruction from God's Word with an attitude that says, "Teach me."

If your attitude toward Scripture is correct, then correct actions can follow. You should "cry for discernment and lift your voice for understanding" (Proverbs 2:3). Amazing statements are made to those who are willing to exert effort to get wisdom. The effort is demonstrated through praying (crying out for wisdom) and studying God's Word as the source of wisdom.

Results of the Search

The first amazing statement in Proverbs is that you will have a relationship with the Lord. You search for wisdom, and you find God. Proverbs 2:5 states, "Then you will discern the fear of the LORD, and discover the knowledge of God." You grow in your understanding of who God is and that he is the necessary foundation upon which you will build the rest of your life. We began this chapter discussing the necessity of building your life on the Lord Jesus Christ, and here it is emphasized again that true wisdom starts with a relationship with the Lord.

Another wonderful result of seeking wisdom relates to your choice of a marriage partner. Proverbs 2:7-8 states that the Lord is a "shield to those who walk in integrity, guarding the paths of justice and he preserves the way of the godly ones." The key principle is that you need to become a lover of the Lord and wisdom before you become a lover of someone else.

God's job is to guard, shield, and preserve those who love his wisdom. Our job is to walk in integrity and to be godly. The Lord promises that this wisdom will help us make decisions that are well considered, and he will guard the decision-making process. When you commit yourself to gaining wisdom, you are more able to discern a person's character and will less likely allow your emotions to lead you astray.

Ladies, please look at these incredible verses. Proverbs 2:12-14 says you will be delivered from "the man who speaks perverse things" those who "walk in the ways of darkness" and "delight in doing evil." Those who walk in darkness have something to hide. Young ladies, you must know what to look for and what to ask yourself concerning a potential mate. Does he ask or expect you to do immoral things? Have you found that he has hidden things from you? What is his reputation? God can give you wisdom to stay away from this type of man.

Gentlemen, check out the next verses. Proverbs 2:16-18 state that this wisdom will "deliver you from the strange woman, from the adulteress who flatters with her words; that leaves the companion of her youth, and forgets the covenant of her God; for her house sinks down to death and her tracks lead to the dead ..." Wisdom can keep you away from a woman who might break her marriage vows. In Proverbs 2:18 the "strange woman" pulls others down spiritually. Ask yourself when considering a mate, does she pull me down spiritually, or does she contribute to my relationship with the Lord?

If you invest time and energy into pursuing wisdom, you will reap the benefits in godly relationships. If you do not invest in wisdom, you will probably reap the consequences of making bad choices in relationships. Over the years, I have dealt with many whose marriage relationships have been broken. None of them had entered marriage believing that they would become a divorce statistic. In one case, the man knew that his future wife had lived a promiscuous life and was not even loyal to him while they were dating; however, his emotions were so focused on her that he married her anyway because he was convinced that he "needed" her. Had this man been committed to learning the principles of wisdom, he would never have married this person. This painful experience has since caused him to progress spiritually, but he could have avoided the experience altogether if he had sought to lay God's wisdom as the foundation of his marriage house.

The time has come to stop accepting weak testimonies. Just because someone goes to church doesn't make him or her a true follower of Christ. Just because someone goes to a Christian college doesn't make him a true follower of Christ. Please commit to the Lord that you will pursue only those who are pursuing him. As has been wisely said, "Run hard after Christ and then look around and see who is running with you. That's the type of person to marry." [20]

If you have already experimented with relationships and have been hurt, humbly turn to God and commit to him your fears. You might pray, "Lord, I am afraid of making a bad choice in a marriage partner. I need your wisdom. I commit myself to pursuing the wisdom that comes from learning the principles that are in your Word. I look forward to the treasures that you reveal to me. I realize that the foundation of my future house must be built with the wisdom that comes only from you, and I commit my life to you. Amen."

Starting to prepare now:

1. What is the evidence in your life that you are a follower of Jesus Christ? If you're not certain, you should review the message of the gospel and commit your life to Christ now.

2. How is your testimony similar or dissimilar to Paul's?

3. Proverbs 8:13 states that those who fear the Lord hate evil or sin. How have you seen this in your life?

4. In what areas of your life do you need to sharpen your hatred of sin?

5. Wisdom is apparent in your relationship choices. How has that wisdom been demonstrated or not demonstrated in your past relationship choices?

6. One who is wise listens to the principles of Scripture. List three ways this is evident in your life.

7. Write a prayer of commitment to the Lord.

Questions to ask about a potential spouse:

1. Is this person pursuing Christ? Is this person a follower of Christ?

2. How would he or she answer the "starting to prepare now" questions?

Chapter 3

GROWING WISER
ABOUT ATTRACTION

A plan in the heart of a man is like deep water, but a
man of understanding draws it out.

Proverbs 20:5

I remember the day that Rose (my future wife) rode by and waved
at me as I was raking leaves at the Bible college we attended. I turned
to a friend who was working beside me and said, "That's a good
sister in the Lord." He looked at me and laughed and said, "Just a
good sister in the Lord? Yeah, right!" He knew by the way that Rose
and I had been talking to each other that this could turn into more
than just a casual relationship. He sensed that we were attracted
to each other. He was right. In a few weeks' time, we became a
"thing" on campus. We had a strong attraction to each other. We
spent lots of time hanging out and talking, and when you saw one
of us, you probably saw the other as well. This leads to the question
I want to address in this chapter—why are people attracted to each
other? Sounds a bit mysterious doesn't it? This is truly a foundational
issue because it has to do with why a relationship even begins. Or,
more accurately, attraction becomes the reason why you would like
a relationship to begin.

After decades of being together, sharing ministry, and parenting six children our marriage is stronger now than ever. We've concluded that good marriages don't just happen, they are made to happen. One of the things that has helped our marriage become stronger has been to understand why we were attracted to each other in the first place. As I think back on it, our initial attraction seems pretty shallow. I just liked that she liked me, and she liked that I was a fun person. Can you see how that could lead to problems? What happens when she stops believing I'm a fun person, or I stop feeling that she likes me?

Couples, of course, are attracted to each other for many reasons. It seems that appearances top the list, at least in American culture. Common interests and athletic ability may also rank high. Another reason may be (like mine), sensing that "This person seems to like me," or, the chemistry just seems right. In other cultures, attraction may be based primarily on things like the ability to provide or on family connections.

Various Views on Attraction

Since at some point relationships involve attraction between two people, doesn't it seem important to understand this phenomenon? To be wise, you need to understand why you are attracted to certain individuals and not to others, and you need to understand where these strong attractions originate. As you begin to think more deeply about this, it will be easy to realize you need wisdom. You can be reassured by what Proverbs 2:10 and 11 states: "For wisdom will enter your heart and knowledge will be pleasant to your soul. Discretion will guard you, understanding will watch over you."

George Bernard Shaw, the Irish playwright, once offered an explanation of attraction.

> Love is an overemphasis on the difference between one person and all others. Once we have discovered that all people are not alike, we begin to have different feelings about different individuals. We feel "better," "happier," or "more powerful" in the presence of others. We wish to spend more time with some and less time (or

perhaps none at all) with others. We can actually sense changes in our bodies when particular people are near us. [21]

Webster's Dictionary defines attraction as "the relationship existing between things or persons that are naturally or involuntarily drawn together. In this chapter I want to explore why this happens. Attraction implies the possession by one thing of a quality that pulls another to it." [22] In other words, there's just something or some things that draw you toward the other person. My mind then naturally asks, what are those things and what is the quality of those things?

Psychological Theories

Psychological theories for attraction abound. One theory is that you subconsciously develop an image of one to whom you will be attracted, possibly combining the positive attributes which you admired in many other people (like a parent). Another popular theory is that you will be attracted to one who will meet your inner needs. Those who hold this idea believe you have a need to be loved or a need for significance or other needs that are driving you. A further theory (growing out of an evolutionary perspective) [23] attributes all of your actions to conscious or unconscious sexual desires. Here is a brief statement that summarizes some of these views:

> The part of your brain that directed your search for a mate … was trying to … re-create the conditions of your upbringing, in order to correct them…. It was attempting to return to the scene of your original frustration so that you could resolve your unfinished business…. Our powers of observation are especially acute when we are looking for a mate, because we are searching for someone to satisfy our fundamental unconscious drives. We subject everyone to the same intense scrutiny: Is this someone who will nurture me and help me recover my lost self? [24]

Understanding Attraction Biblically

As you can see, many explanations for attraction assume there is a subconscious part of you that you don't consciously know is influencing you. But, according to Scripture a heart shaped by what happened in Genesis 3 with the Fall is the primary influencer. "The heart is more deceitful than all else and is desperately sick, who can understand it" (Jeremiah 17:9). I'm sure there are other ingredients to attraction not addressed in this chapter (e.g., God's sovereign leading), but I'm equally convinced that what we are about to study plays a significant role.

You may ask, "Can't I just trust the way my heart is feeling about someone?" Biblically the wise answer must be, "NO!" Because young people tend to be too trustful of their inner persons and have not developed a wise heart as Proverbs 2 encourages, there has been much devastation in marriage. Culture says, "Let your heart be your guide." Scripture says, "Watch over your heart with all diligence for from it flow the springs of life" (Proverbs 4:23).

This can be reduced to some very simple advice if you want to be biblically wise. Be careful of how your heart (inner person) is leading you. I know that sounds like strange advice for romantic relationships.

Strong Desires

I believe Scripture presents truth amid a world of theory. It is all right to want a special someone to be strongly attracted to you, and it is all right for you to be strongly attracted to someone special as long as the reasons for your attractions are correct. Scripture vividly describes two people who are passionately in love with each other; the bride says of her bridegroom, "His mouth is full of sweetness. And he is *wholly desirable* (emphasis added). This is my beloved and this is my friend …" (Song of Solomon 5:16) The bridegroom says that his bride is the "most beautiful among women" (Song of Solomon 1:8b). They were strongly attracted to each other!

That's what the Hebrew word *chamad*, translated "wholly desirable," means. It is the same word used in Isaiah 53:2, which says, "He has no stately form or majesty that we should look upon

Him, nor appearance that we should be *attracted* to Him." [emphasis added] This verse is speaking about our Savior, the Messiah, and how people were not attracted to him after he was physically marred by the events of the crucifixion. In fact, he probably looked repulsive after undergoing so much torture because of our sin. Please hold on to the thought that "attraction" has to do with "desires."

Before we move on, please notice how the girl in Song of Solomon talks about him as her friend. Many couples have mainly, or only, physical attraction motivating the relationship and have never learned how to be friends. As you probably realize, physical attraction alone leads to a weak foundation for a future marriage house. But being attracted to other qualities including good relationship skills (like communication and just knowing how to be a friend) is necessary to form a strong structure for your marriage house.

Not All Desires are Sinful

Does this mean that all the things we are attracted to are sinful? Some are strongly attracted to sports, others to a hobby, others to money. The list could go on and on. The problem is not necessarily the object (unless it is something intrinsically evil like porn). The problem is what your desires, which have been influenced by sin, do with this attraction. For example, are you more passionate about whatever you are attracted to than your relationship with the Lord? Unfortunately, for all of us, the answer is yes many times. Sin distorts our desires. Good things turn bad or get out of balance. These are strong words, but it is vital that you really understand what these attractions represent in your inner being, what Scripture calls your heart. Are you seeing how attraction and desire are directly related?

Let's think then about how we can know if strong attraction has the right motives or wrong motives. In Ezekiel 23:11-12, God is condemning Jerusalem (i.e., its people) for her spiritual unfaithfulness to him and calls her actions "harlotry." She was like the woman Oholibah, who had strong desires for the Assyrians instead of for God. Verse 12 states, "She lusted after the Assyrian governors and officials, the ones near, magnificently dressed, horsemen riding on horses, all of them desirable [*chamad*] young men." Notice again that this is the same word as attraction.

Jerusalem was considered an adulterous wife because she was strongly attracted to the wrong people and the wrong things. Her focus was on only the outward appearance, and they were Assyrians! This strong desire caused her to forget that the Assyrians represented worship of false gods.

We can learn lessons from Jerusalem's actions. If someone is delightful to the eyes and desirable, wouldn't it be wise to ask yourself, "Why am I attracted to this person? What do I want from this person?" Please notice the word "want." This term helps us get a biblical understanding of what is happening in attraction. By accepting this, you will be growing in insight regarding what is happening during attraction.

This doesn't mean you have to marry someone you would consider unattractive or that being attracted to physical beauty is all wrong. Aren't you glad I clarified that! Our sin nature can blow physical attraction out of proportion though, and Scripture warns us that this is not to be the first priority (Proverbs 31:30). God made us to enjoy beauty, but our inner person distorts it. A typical example would be pornography. God made the sexual relationship to be beautiful for a husband and wife, but pornography distorts and exploits the beauty of the body. God has given us an intrinsic delight in beautiful things, but wisdom would tell us that beauty must not be the only or even the chief priority in determining attraction.

Desire has gotten a whole lot of people in trouble. In fact, that is how all of us got in trouble originally. This same Hebrew word is used in Genesis to describe how we ended up with the sinful desires we have. "When the woman saw that the tree was good for food, and that it was a delight to the eyes, and that the tree was *desirable* [emphasis added] to make one wise, she took from its fruit and ate; and she gave also to her husband with her, and he ate" (Genesis 3:6). This passage ought to clearly warn us that, just because someone is delightful to the eyes and desirable, it still may not be wise to have a relationship with him or her. In fact, usually it is not wise if you are the type of person who has a track record of living by what naturally attracts you, instead of developing the type of discernment that Proverbs 2 encourages.

As we said before and now putting it bluntly—just the fact that you are attracted to someone does not make it right. A wise person would ask himself or herself, "Why am I attracted to this person?" "What is it I want?" "What is going on with my desires?"

Just as Jerusalem reaped serious consequences because of her ungodly desires, our strong desires for ungodly people and inappropriate things can create devastation in our lives. Living by what naturally attracts us, without developing godly wisdom to know what should attract us, is a dangerous way to live. I believe this is a reason so many marriages end up in trouble.

Understanding the Heart

It ought to be clear by now that attraction is directly related to desires, and the Bible tells us that desires are directly related to our heart. According to Scripture, your heart is your whole inner person with your thoughts, discernment, and emotions. [25] In other words, your decisions reflect your heart. Your emotions reflect your heart and your thinking mirrors your heart. All three of these areas are windows into the heart. This means that emotions are a peek into the inner person. Your thinking reveals your inner person, and your decision-making reveals who you are on the inside. If this is true, I'm sure you can see why it is so important to understand the heart in romantic relationships, since so often your mind is obsessed with the other person. Your emotions get easily stirred up in romantic relationships, and your will or decision-making ability is definitely impacted. In fact, I've heard of people making pretty erratic decisions because of a romantic relationship. Like the guy who missed his fiancée so much that he made a quick decision to pack and drive 700 miles all night to Chicago to see her. He fell asleep numerous times while driving and even passed a car and didn't remember doing so. Emotion and desire clearly affected his thinking and decisions. By the way, that person was me (blush)!

This becomes more clear with the help of Hebrews 4:12 when it tells us that our hearts have "thoughts and intentions." [26] My imaginings and what I intend on doing, or plan on doing, or resolve to do are all part of my heart. It is easy to see how this relates to romantic relationships, and this answers some key questions about attraction, such as "What do I want?" Or, "What am I looking for in relationships?" Or, maybe the most convicting question is, "What do my desires tell me about where my heart is?"

The Heart Is the Center of Worship

To give you extra motivation to work on understanding your heart, you need to understand that it is fundamentally about worship. This is essential to know, since it is easy to have an out-of-balance perspective on another person in romantic relationships. We easily end up worshiping and serving another person rather than the Creator (Romans 1:25). I see this happening with couples all too frequently and it does nothing but add tremendous pressure to the relationship since one person has to live up to the other's high expectations for the relationship.

It is easy to demonstrate that the idea of the heart and worship are tied together. In Matthew 12:34-35 the Lord is challenging the religious leaders about what was happening in their inner persons. He says, "For the mouth speaks out of that which fills the heart. The good man out of his good treasure brings forth what is good." Note that the Lord uses treasure as a synonym for the heart. My heart is about my treasures. Let's put this all together with worship and romantic relationships. The Old English word for worship is *"worthship."* What I think is worth my time and energy demonstrates the treasures of my inner person. Whatever stirs my emotions and motivates me to make decisions reveals my inner person. Can you see how romantic relationships often reveal the true worship of the heart? Who or what is captivating your inner person? As we saw in the last chapter, you were made for this to be primarily the Lord.

Psalm 18 Helps Us Understand [27]

In this beautiful psalm, David is describing his intimacy with the Lord while under attack. The first verses in particular are picturesque as he states this vital relationship with the LORD who is his Rock, Fortress, Deliverer, and Refuge. David illustrates that the LORD is to be these things for us. He is to be our security and the One we run to when dealing with the pressure of life. I often encounter young people who think getting married is the answer to life, or who think if someone just liked them, then life would feel so much better. Romantic relationships are notorious for becoming unstable rocks, refuges and deliverers.

Can my wife be a legitimate source of security for me? Of course she can, as long as she is not the chief source. She can be a refuge for me as long as she is not the main refuge. Making another fallen person your chief security leads to nothing but frustration, anger and disappointment because they can't be God. It is easy to put another person on a pedestal to supposedly meet all your needs or to yearn for a human relationship to meet all your needs. But, it can't happen! Another human was not made to do this, and this is especially true since Genesis 3.

Stuart Scott, in his excellent book *The Exemplary Husband*, describes what happens when a person has the wrong view of love for others.

> For some, a sense of great *need* is the prevailing attraction toward another person. The needy person may feel as if he or she cannot live without the relationship, and they may become desperate at the thought of losing it. In this case, they are gaining something from the other person that they feel they desperately need. Actually this neediness is more selfish than it is loving. Needing is *not* the same as loving (1 Corinthians 13:5b). [28]

In reality what seems like neediness is actually parasitic. One or both are living off another. To have healthy relationships you must have a proper perspective on other human relationships, and learn to make the Lord your chief refuge and strength, and not others. If you put others in the chief place of filling some void in your life, in actuality what you have done is put them on a pedestal to have god-like status. That would be idolatrous desire just as we saw in Ezekiel.

Keeping Our Loves in Order

In Matthew 22: 36-40 our Lord states some principles that can help us keep relationships in their proper place. When asked, "Which is the great commandment in the Law?" He answered by stating that the greatest commandment is not one of the Ten Commandments, but instead, "'You shall love the LORD your God with all your heart, and with all your soul, and with all your mind' ... And a second is like it, 'You shall love your neighbor as yourself.'" Notice two things; love for the Lord is primary, and it is a love that captivates the whole person just as other romantic relationships captivate. He is to be chief. Secondly, the two great commandments cannot be placed side by side. Loving others must be in submission to love for the Lord. What would we call it if someone loves another at the same level as his or her love for the Lord? That's right, it's idolatry. To protect ourselves from this we must love others based on a relationship with the Lord.

Let me demonstrate the beauty of this principle, and I know it will come in handy in the future. If you love others out of your love, commitment, and devotion to the Lord, then you will find it a whole lot easier to love the person not just because of who he or she is, but even in spite of who he or she is. In others words, when the person is being difficult to love (and I assure you there will be those times), then you can still love them because of your even deeper commitment to the Lord.

A wise person will analyze his or her feelings of attraction as desires, and do this in the light of God's Word. These feelings are wrong only when they lead to disobedience to what the Lord commands in his Word (for example, sex outside of marriage), or if these feelings replace your love for the Lord of the Word. An example of this would be that strong sexual desires for your mate are right and proper according to the Song of Solomon; however, these desires must be fulfilled scripturally—only in marriage. "Marriage is to be held in honor among all, and the marriage bed is to be undefiled, for fornicators and adulterers God will judge" (Hebrews 13:4).

If you want to be sure that the attraction you feel for someone is right, ask yourself questions like the following:

- Is my attraction just for the physical, or am I attracted to who this person is spiritually as well?

- Is this attraction more important than my relationship with the Lord?

- Am I attracted to this person out of some sense of neediness?

I hope you find all this as reassuring as I do. David says in Psalm 63:8 that it is possible to have a satisfying, passionate relationship with the Lord. "My soul clings to You; Your right hand upholds me." I believe this means we must pursue relationship with him primarily as our Rock and not other relationships. Who or what we trust in, is a decision we must make everyday. Augustine wrote: "You have made man for yourself and restless is the human heart until it comes to rest in you." [29] Think of how solid marriages would be if both individuals had this kind of relationship with the Lord.

Let's Practice

To practice a biblical view of understanding attraction and worship, let's look at the chart below from a high school marriage preparation textbook titled, *Building Relationships*.

Premarital Fantasies and Marital Realities

She married him because he was such an assertive male;
She divorced him because he was such a domineering husband.

He married her because she was so gentle and petite;
He divorced her because she was so weak and helpless.

She married him because he could provide a good income;
She divorced him because all he did was work.

He married her because she was so attractive all the time;
He divorced her because she spent too much time in front of the mirror.

She married him because he was so romantic and sociable;
She divorced him because he was such a fun-loving playboy.

He married her because she was so quiet and dependant;
He divorced her because she was so boring and clinging.

She married him because he was the life of the party;
She divorced him because he was such a dud at home.

He married her because she was so sociable and talkative;
He divorced her because she could only discuss trivia.

She married him because he was such a good athlete;
She divorced him because he was either playing or watching sports.

He married her because she was so neat and organized;
He divorced her because she was too compulsive and controlling.

Following this chart, the authors state,

> In one of life's puzzles, partners often become more critical and less accepting of each other after marriage. When we love and marry someone, our love should ensure a certain amount of respect and civility in the relationship. But we often treat strangers on the street and friends with more respect and tolerance than we do our partner. [30]

Let's see if we can understand the heart's motivation for several of these marriage relationships, and perhaps we can solve what these authors think is "one of life's puzzles."

In the first scenario, "She married him because he was such an assertive male." Remember that the heart motivations are revealed by what a person desires. So, what was she lusting for? Maybe it was that she wanted a strong man to protect her? I would call this "comfort or security idolatry." And as is typical, her desires disappointed her. Scripture says that disappointment will come to those who worship something or someone other than the Lord (Proverbs 1:29-33).

Let me be clear though, the idea of having a strong husband is not wrong. The problem comes when you think you *must* have a strong husband to make it through life or when this is the ruling desire of your heart. Well then, how do you identify a ruling desire? The answer—what captivates your thinking? What does your inner person meditate on?

Perhaps this woman relished what others thought of her when they saw her with such a strong man. Scripture calls this people pleasing or the fear of man. Whatever her motivations, her desires led her astray. The very thing that attracted her to him she now finds repulsive because sinful desires disappoint, and divorce followed.

Consider the third scenario on the chart. "She married him because he could provide a good income." She is probably worshiping or desiring money and materialism. Or, perhaps she likes the status that being married to this man gives her. Matthew 6:24 states, "No one can serve two masters; for either he will hate the one and love the other, or he will hold to the one and despise the other. You cannot serve God and mammon [materialism]."

Desires like this, that are out-of-balance, place responsibilities on the potential spouse that God never intended for them to carry. If we understand that individuals enter marriage with wrong expectations because they want the other partner to be something that only God can be, then it is no shock that they become disappointed and critical.

The contrast is always between what we are wanting, serving, and seeking, and our wanting, serving, and seeking the Lord. You were created to be a worshiper. The crucial question is what or whom are you going to worship?

Heart Idolatries

The following are the heart idolatries that I typically encounter while doing premarital counseling. See if you find yourself in this list.

1. **Control:** "I have to know the future to be happy." "Life is all right if my life is organized and I have it under control."

2. **Pleasure:** "Life is about having fun." "I need to hang around people who like to have fun." "The way to handle the pressures of life is by giving myself some pleasure."

3. **Keeping people happy:** "I am very concerned about what people think about me." "I have to make sure that I look good." "I must avoid conflicts." "There are some people that I am really afraid of."

4. **Success:** "I must be successful." "I am pursuing this degree because it will help me make a lot of money and make me look successful." "I must dress a certain way to make me look successful."

5. **Material things:** "The way to be happy is to be able to buy things." "It makes me feel good to shop."

6. **Money:** "I need money to be secure."

7. **Comfort:** "Life's about taking it easy and relaxing."

Enjoying life is no sin; the LORD desires us to enjoy life. The sin is in worshiping the gifts of God instead of the God who gives the gifts. "Instruct those who are rich in this present world not to be conceited or to fix their hope on the uncertainty of riches, but on God, who richly supplies us with all things to enjoy" (1 Timothy 6:17). The key is to enjoy life and what it contains as an act of worship (1 Corinthians 10:31).

A Case Study: Terri and George

Terri and George, who had recently become engaged, came to me for premarital counseling. During the counseling it became obvious that Terri's guilt about her sexual past (before her relationship with George) dominated her. She felt unworthy and guilty about her love and strong physical attraction for George. Because he was such a godly man, she wondered if her motivations for a relationship with him were proper.

I saw that before they could build a solid marriage, Terri had to grow in maturity and with the help of biblical principles deal with her fear of rejection, feelings of unworthiness, guilt over past sins, love of seeking pleasure, and desire to control others. So I advised them to postpone their wedding.

In order to help Terri fully understand God's forgiveness through the gospel, and to help her understand what created her "baggage," I asked her to answer the following questions and statements. Notice how all relate to the mind, will, or emotions. In other words, they are about her heart. It was important for her to understand what led her to these past sins so that she would not repeat the same patterns with George.

1. When do you tend to experience fear, worry, or anxiety?
2. In what areas have you struggled with disappointment?
3. In what situations do you struggle with anger?
4. What things do you find yourself seeking to avoid?
5. Whose opinion really matters to you?
6. Life would be all right if _____.
7. I really wish I had_____.
8. I need_____.

I was trying to help Terri understand "the thoughts and intentions" of her heart (Hebrews 4:12). Why was she attracted to her previous boyfriend to begin with? What were her heart's intentions for a relationship? Maybe seeing what she wrote will help you understand your own motivations.

Here is how she answered question three. "I struggle with anger when I do not have control over a situation in my life." And answering question four she wrote, "I tend to put up walls with others so that I will not get hurt. I do not tell others what is really on my mind and heart because of fear of man."

What is ruling her heart? She wrote the following when she filled in the blank of the statement, "Life would be all right if_____." "Life would always be great if things were always under control and if I knew others always liked me." What are the desires of her heart? *She was living to control her own life and to keep people happy.*

She wanted to keep people happy all the time, especially people she thought she needed something from (like her previous boyfriend). We also found out she was highly motivated to seek pleasure. She thought this would bring her satisfaction in life, but instead it brought her great pain, especially when her previous boyfriend started to abuse her physically. Because these types of things were ruling desires, she was willing to be in a sexual relationship with him to keep him happy. She did not want to lose him.

These questions helped to unveil what was lurking in her inner person. Terri's answers proved that she wanted control over her life, that she put up walls between her and others so she would not get hurt, that she would not tell others what was really on her mind because of fear of others, and that she wanted to be liked by everyone. She realized that her past decisions came from a heart that worshiped the wrong things—pleasure, control, and approval were dominant themes. When she asked the Lord's forgiveness and began a passionate relationship with him first, he replaced the idols with love, peace, purity, wisdom, grace, and true pleasure.

If false worship is the problem, then true worship is the solution. For Terri this meant:

1. To deal with her desires for control, she needed to choose to trust the Lord on an active daily basis. That's living as a worshiper.

2. To grow away from her people-pleasing tendencies that had led to so much sin in her life, she needed to grow in awe of her Lord and not be overawed by other people. This is something she worked on daily and she grew! That's living as a worshiper.

3. As an act of worship, she needed to accept the forgiveness that is in Christ. I'm happy to report that the Lord helped her grow as she endeavored to live as a worshiper of the Lord as her chief priority.

She and George are now happily married. They have children they are raising for the Lord and have led significant ministries at their church. You too can learn to grow in discerning what is happening in your heart, and as you do, you will have a clearer understanding of your attractions.

Starting to prepare now:

Note: By carefully answering the following questions, just as Terri did, you can examine the thoughts, motives and desires of your heart.

You will begin to see how these desires have shaped your true treasures, and you will see how they have shaped the way that you have responded to God, others, and the situations of life. If you have a mentor, maybe he or she could help you understand the patterns you see in your life.

1. When do you tend to experience fear, worry, or anxiety? (Matthew 19:34).

2. In what area have you struggled with disappointment? (Proverbs 13:12, 19).

3. In what situations do you struggle with anger? (James 4:1, 2; Proverbs 11:23).

4. Where do you encounter problems in relationships? (James 4: 1-10).

5. What are the situations of life that you find particularly difficult? (1 Corinthians 10:13,14).

6. What kinds of things do you find yourself trying to avoid?

7. In what way have you experienced regular problems in your relationship with the Lord?

8. In what situations do you tend to doubt the truths of Scripture?

9. What is a good relationship? What do you expect of others?

10. In what situations do you struggle with bitterness?

11. When have you struggled with regret, being tempted to say, "if only_____?

12. What experiences from the past do you have a hard time letting go of?

13. In what area do you tend to struggle with envy? What do you find yourself wanting that others have?

14. Whose opinions really matter to you?

Fill in the Blanks

1. Life would be all right if_____?

2. I really wish I had_____?

3. I need_____?

Adapted from *The Journal of Biblical Counseling,* Fall 1996.

Now that you have answered these questions, work back through your responses looking for patterns. What do your answers tell you about what you are wanting in life? To what do you seem devoted? What seems to be a strong desire for you?

What word or phrase captures these desires? (Hint: you may see more than one pattern). Do you desire to control life? How about keeping people happy? How could these desires influence the type of person to whom you may be attracted?

What can you do to replace false worship with true worship? How could growing in love for the Lord and others help replace the false worship in your heart? What would this look like day to day?

In Appendix 2 you will find a "marriage preparation project." Answering these questions well is foundational to that practical project.

Questions to ask about a potential spouse:

How would someone you are considering as a husband or wife answer these questions?

Chapter 4

GOD'S WISE DESIGN FOR MARRIAGE

For this cause a man shall leave his father and his mother, and shall cleave to his wife; and they shall become one flesh.

Genesis 2:24

I have many memories of sketches and plans for buildings in my dad's office. He designed buildings for Christian camps and the plans for a whole apartment complex. He also designed the home we lived in during my teenage years. It was common to see rolls of blueprints around the house or in the car. Blueprints are the pages of exact plans for every aspect of the building. They include plans for plumbing and electric as well as where walls and doors will be located. When it was time to build the project we followed the plan. I do remember a time or two when someone didn't look at the plan precisely enough; we ended up having to tear out a wall that was put in the wrong place!

Everything by Design

Since God is the Creator of the universe, he also does everything by design. Think of his plans as that of an architect. The architect comes up with plans for a home and expects the builder to follow the blueprints. If the blueprints are followed, then the home is constructed properly. If the plans are not followed, well, you have a mess.

In many cultures some have the opinion that there is something wrong with the concept of marriage. They have never (or rarely) seen a good marriage, but have seen so many examples of bad marriages that they believe that the idea of marriage itself is the problem. I've actually had people say in counseling, "If God came up with the idea of marriage, he must be a cruel God." Yet, could it be that there is so much pain because couples build upon their own foundation for marriage and not his? Could it be that many people marry without knowing what the Designer intended? Doesn't it make sense that homes and families that become wrecks are those not built using the blueprints of the Designer? The answer to the problems we are seeing in marriage is not to abandon the idea of marriage, but to start to rebuild marriage in the way God intended. The problem is not with the design; it's that we are ignoring the Designer. This chapter is written with the conviction that God's ways really do work.

The Wrong Blueprint

Before looking at the Designer's original intentions, let's think about why some people do get married, and why marriage matters. Many marry because it's what you do when you are attracted to someone. Others marry as a way to get away from a bad home situation. I once had a woman tell me that the reason she married her husband was because she knew he would be successful and he would provide nice things for her. Sounds really romantic, doesn't it?

Others have unrealistic expectations of marriage, and they marry trying to find their chief significance and security in the relationship. These reasons create marriages in which each mate can be overly dependent on the other for fulfilling these needs. This will surely lead to an incorrectly built house. When the mate fails (and he or she will), great disappointment will follow. As we saw in the last chapter, the Psalms often calls the Lord our "rock" and our "refuge" and warns us not to put our chief trust in people (Psalm 146:3). Seeking your chief security and significance in the Lord helps to guard against unrealistic expectations in marriage.

God's Original Design

Before we discuss God's original design, we need to look at something quite basic. In some cultures, things have become so antagonistic toward a traditional view of marriage that we should take a little time to discuss why marriage matters.

Why Marriage Matters

Fundamentally, marriage matters because God says it matters, but here are some other benefits which can be backed up by sociological research. [31]

1.   Bonding, intimacy, and true friendship come through the commitment of marriage. This was God's design for "one fleshness."

2.   Marriage leads to the stability of society. For example, did you know that men who are married tend to work harder than un-married men? This is obviously good for any society.

3.   Marriage leads to stability for children—children from intact homes with a mother and father are much more stable than those from a single parent or broken home.

4.   Think of this one. You get to live life with a committed "teammate" rather than navigating life on your own. (I really like this!)

5.   Marriage leads to a healthier life as husband and wife care for one another.

6.   Marriage creates many satisfying memories. Some of my favorites are sitting around the dinner table and talking and laughing together on one of our many camping trips.

7.   Marriage also allows you to serve as teammates in ministry as you reflect the glory of God together.

In summary, "On average, married couples are happier, healthier, wealthier, enjoy longer lives, and report greater sexual satisfaction than single, divorced, or cohabiting individuals." [32]

I find all of this very encouraging and this list reminds me why I like family life so much. But ultimately, marriage matters because it is a picture of our Lord's relationship with his church. This reason alone is enough for the church to say that marriage matters.

It's time now to turn our attention to God's blueprints for marriage and to look in Scripture to see where he gives us that plan.

Chapters 1 and 2 of Genesis show the very foundations of God's purposes for marriage. In fact, these chapters show the foundation of everything. They give a framework for life, demonstrating where the natural world came from, how we got here, where emotions of fear and shame originate, and even why we wear clothing! As you begin to understand God's blueprint, I hope you will only look for someone who holds the same beliefs about the meaning of marriage.

Reflecting the Image of God in Man (Genesis 1:26-27)

It seems logical to start with the first chapter of Genesis. Near the end of the chapter the Lord gives us his first intentions for marriage. Then God said, "Let us make man in Our image, according to Our likeness; and let them rule over the fish of the sea and over the birds of the sky and over the cattle and over all the earth, and over every creeping thing that creeps on the earth. And God created man in His own image, in the image of God He created Him; male and female He created them."

We have the high calling of bearing the image of God on earth. He spoke everything else into existence, but he breathed the breath of God into man (Genesis 2:7). The special effort that created mankind as distinct from animals gives mankind unique value and dignity. This high calling has a direct application for the way a married couple should treat each other. One is not better than the other; both are created in the image of God and should be treated and spoken to with respect.

What does it mean to be "in the image of God," or to put it more clearly, to image God? Every part of our being is a reflection of some aspect of God, and we carry in our body a vivid reminder of who he is. All human characteristics were originally created to reflect God, and to give him glory. For example, he sees and he has strength, so we see and have strength. Something radical happened though due to the fall (chapter 3) and we do not reflect glory back to him. In fact, we more often than not want to reflect glory back to ourselves. The good news is that our Savior died so that the image of God in man could be restored (Colossians 3:10).

To have a better understanding, we must think of Jesus, the One who perfectly pictured God on earth because he *was* God on earth. It is reassuring to realize that as you grow in your relationship with him, you are becoming more "godly" or "Godlike." Think of the amazing potential a married couple have as they grow in Christlikeness together. To say a couple has a godly marriage is really to say they have a Christlike marriage.

How is the image of God reflected in marriage? When God said, "Let us make man in our image" (1:26), the "us" and "our" are the first hint of the Trinity in the Bible. Obviously the members of the Trinity are in perfect relationship with one another. So mankind, individually and together, reflects the image of God. Part of image bearing is being in relationship with one another. But marriage provides a unique opportunity to glorify God when the husband and wife are in a redeemed relationship reflecting his image. This seems to be the implication of God in making them male and female. In other words, he receives glory when a couple live their married life displaying godly love and wisdom. In any culture a couple who lives for the glory of God instead of their own glory will stand out as unique. [33]

Let's turn now to Genesis 2 and see another part of the Architect's design.

Not Good for Man to Be Alone (2:18)

"Then the LORD God said, 'It is not good for man to be alone; I will make him a helper suitable for him.'" Let's look at the broader context of this verse and by doing so, I believe your view of marriage will be elevated. For the first time in the creation process God said something was *not* good. After every other day he had said it was "good." Why isn't it good like everything else? Well, because Adam didn't have his companion. The Lord already knew what he would do, and accordingly the last creative act of God was to make woman— the pinnacle of creation. How do you like that, ladies? Then the last action of God during this creation week was to bring the man and woman together in the marriage union. Thus, we can legitimately say that marriage is the crowning action of creation. This is particularly significant when you realize that these chapters are not chronological. Chapter 2 is actually part of day six of creation. It fills in details that the end of chapter 1 does not have. Then, after God creates the woman and starts marriage he says, "it was *very* good" (verse 31). Now doesn't that give you a higher view of marriage?

Adam needed a companion in order for God to say that his creation was now very good. After Adam named all of the animals, "there was not found a helper suitable to him." The words "was not found" are interesting. God was not doing the searching, Adam was. God's object lesson worked, and Adam realized as he looked that he was alone and did not have a mate as the animals did. The emphasis is not that Adam was lonely, but that creation was not complete until Adam and Eve were united to live in relationship with one another and fulfill God's purposes for them as a team. [34]

Let's look more deeply into one aspect of a proper husband and wife relationship. We already learned many helpful things from Proverbs 2, but let's add to the list. Proverbs 2:17 introduced us to the woman who left the *companion* of her youth. She was not an honorable woman because she broke her marriage vows by committing adultery, and God views this as a great sin. I have seen the tremendous pain that is caused when a spouse abandons his or her partner. A young woman whose husband had abandoned her said to me, "I feel like I have lost my best friend." That's not surprising when you understand what the Hebrew word for companion means.

The word actually means friend. It is also the same word in Hebrew for cattle. [35] It may sound strange but could there be a connection between the meanings of these two words? One source defines the word this way, "The primary sense is that of one who is always in company with another, i.e., a guide or companion or friend." [36] The possible connection between the word friend and cattle is logical when you remember that, as an agricultural society, Israel would have yoked cattle together for work purposes. This yoking together may have become the symbol of friendship. In friendship there is teamwork where one complements the other's weaknesses and both work on projects together. Your mate is to be your best friend, your most intimate friend, because sexual attraction alone will not hold a marriage together.

When looking for a spouse isn't it practical to just ask yourself, "Can I truly be friends with this person?" Are you attracted to the person because of their qualities of friendship?

Unfortunately, many marriages have never included the basic ingredient of friendship because their relationships are built only on sexual attraction. Their desires tell them that they like someone, but these desires are primarily for the physical. It is not because of common interests, the ability to talk intimately with someone, or the characteristics that make up friendship.

Children

There are other implications of the phrase "it is not good for man to be alone." God had intentions for marriage that man could not accomplish by himself. One of these intentions was for the man and the woman to have children. Genesis 1:28 makes this clear. It's a shame that many would view children as a hindrance when Scripture teaches they are a great blessing and can bind a marriage together.

God never intended children to be the product of a non-married person's sexual life or to be reared by one parent. No wonder there is so much turmoil in the lives of many children. God does give grace and wisdom to those single parents who are Christians and who are relying on him; however, this situation is not his original intention. [37]

Covenant Relationship

Another reason Adam could not be by himself was that God planned for marriage to picture our Savior's relationship with the church, his bride. In Ephesians 5:21-33, Paul compares marriage to Christ's relationship with the church. In verse 21 Paul quotes from Genesis 2:24, and in verse 32 he says, "This mystery is great; but I am speaking with reference to Christ and the church." A mystery is something that happens in which not all the facts are known. Paul is clearing up the mystery about marriage. He uses the word "mystery" earlier in Ephesians and again in Ephesians 3:3-6. He is referring to the church, the bride of Christ. Moses did not know all of God's intentions when he wrote Genesis 2, but Paul did. God's intention from the beginning was for a marriage to picture the loving relationship Christ would have with his church.

It is amazing to think about how deep this relationship is to be. The depth becomes clear when you realize Christ's relationship with the church is based on a covenant. The Lord said at the Last Supper, which is the basis of our communion service, "This cup is the new covenant in my blood ..." (1 Corinthians 11:24). Earlier in chapter 10, verse 16, Paul said, "Is not the cup of blessing which we bless a sharing in the blood of Christ?" These verses indicate that when we receive Christ as Savior, we become one flesh with him, and we enter into a covenant relationship.

What do we mean by marriage being a covenant relationship? Proverbs 2 can help us answer the question. In Proverbs 2:17 the woman is condemned because she "leaves the *companion* of her youth, and forgets the *covenant* of her God." The phrase "covenant of her God" seems to refer to her marriage. Malachi 2:14 uses the same word to describe marriage and expresses God's displeasure with Judah for breaking his marriage vows, "the LORD has been a witness between you and the wife of your youth, against whom you have dealt treacherously, though she is your *companion* and your wife by *covenant*." The Lord was very upset with them for breaking their marriage covenant in the vows that they had taken before God. Because he takes covenants seriously, it ought to be clear that we should also.

Let's explore this idea of marriage being a covenant relationship created to picture Christ's relationship with the church. The word *covenant* in its basic form means "to cut." [38] It was used for serious formal agreements being made in the Old Testament. The *Theological Wordbook of the Old Testament* describes this ceremony as "accompanied by signs, sacrifices, and a solemn oath that sealed the relationship with promises of blessing for keeping the covenant and curses for breaking it." [39] Jay Adams describes this well;

> All these facts make it clear as can be that marriage is fundamentally a contractual arrangement (called in Mal. 2:14 a marriage "by covenant") and not a sexual union. Marriage is a formal (covenant) arrangement between two persons to become each other's loving companions for life.... Our modern wedding ceremonies should stress this point more fully than they do. [40]

If this is true, then the covenant is made at the ceremony as the vows are exchanged. God is there as a witness hearing the vows, and when the pastor says, "I now pronounce you husband and wife," God agrees that they are husband and wife. The sexual relationship is a symbol of what has already been agreed upon. To summarize, we could define marriage then as "a covenant of companionship." [41] It is more than this, but not less than this. It ought to be clear that it is serious and lifelong, and there are consequences for breaking the covenant.

Marriage serves a larger purpose than two coming together because they feel in love and are seeking to be each other's "soul mate." There are deep eternal purposes going on that should sober and also excite us.

As you prepare for marriage, please understand that God has a purpose and plan for your marriage to be a gospel presentation to the world. You will be demonstrating the type of love that Christ showed by dying for his bride (the church), and the type of love the bride has by living for the Groom (Christ). You must rid your mind of your own selfish purposes for marriage and replace them with God's purposes if you want to marry wisely and well. Marriage is a wonderful experience for those couples who live by God's blueprint and not by their own. As you grow in the acceptance of God's plan, you will experience the beauty of marriage as God designed and ordained it.

Completer (Genesis 2:18)

Sadly, many cultures have rejected or become uncomfortable with what the Bible teaches about male and female roles in marriage. According to Scripture, the husband fulfills the role of Christ in the relationship (Ephesians 5:23, 25). He is definitely the loving leader in the relationship. The wife fulfills the role of the church (Ephesians 5:24-25). The church follows the leadership of the "head," Christ. She is loved and cherished by her husband, but she is not equal in authority because only one can be the chief decision maker.

According to his purposes for marriage, God designed the man to lovingly lead and the wife to lovingly support. Eve was created to be Adam's "helper suitable." I know this can be an uncomfortable truth, but Scripture makes clear that she found her fulfillment in completing him. As each one fulfills his and her God-given role, together they bring glory to the Lord who gives stability to the relationship built according to his blueprint.

Let's think in more detail about these roles. Ephesians 5:25-32 lays the groundwork for the man's role of loving leadership. This pattern for men is Christ's sacrificial love for his bride, the church. This love is also pictured in Genesis 2 as Adam literally gave of himself for his future wife. God carefully formed Adam's body out of the ground, and then the woman was carefully formed from Adam. Woman is of the same substance, but she is specifically formed as a gift to man. They are equal in substance and essence, but different in their roles.

Accepting God's design for roles leads to wisdom because you'll be doing things God's way, not your own. This then helps you become wiser in who you pursue for marriage because it teaches you to ask questions like these: "Is this a man I can lovingly support and follow?" "Is this a woman who would be supportive of my calling in life?" Or, "Can I see myself sacrificially loving this person for life?" Asking wise questions is much better than building a relationship on the inadequate foundation of just emotion or a sexual relationship, and then having the relationship crumble or develop cracks when you discover (as many do) that you did not really know that person.

Deep Intimacy (Genesis 2:23, 24)

Genesis 2:21-22 records the first surgery and the first marriage in history—both performed by God——and also tells how deeply intimate the marriage relationship is designed to be. Verse 21 says, "So the Lord God caused a deep sleep to fall upon the man, and he slept; then He took one of his ribs, and closed up the flesh at that place. And the Lord God fashioned into a woman the rib which He had taken from the man, and brought her to the man."

Adam and Eve had a one-flesh relationship. Eve was *literally* the "flesh and blood" of Adam. This closeness is our Creator's desire for all marriages. Adam describes their closeness well when he said, "This is now bone of my bone and flesh of my flesh...." He then names her "woman," which means "from man." Even her name reinforces how intimate this relationship is to be! Moses then adds the verse that Paul later quotes in Ephesians 5, "For this cause a man shall leave his father and his mother and shall cleave to his wife; and they shall become one flesh."

This intense personal relationship is to be much more than a sexual one. It is sexual and passionately so (just read the Song of Solomon to see what Scripture portrays as okay between a husband and wife). The term "one flesh" is also symbolic, as is shown in 2 Samuel 5:1. There the people of Israel tell David that they want to be his bone and his flesh. What are they endeavoring to communicate? "David, we want to be completely loyal and totally identified with you." This is the meaning of a husband and wife as "one flesh."

In other words, part of "one fleshness" is knowing each other at the deepest level and still being committed to each other. *This leads to loving someone because of who he or she is and in spite of who he or she is.* This can then lead to true intimacy. We ought to be able to say, "I know your heart's tendencies (using the term as we did in the last chapter) and I still love you." They should become so close that they can tell each other their deepest temptations, and commit to helping each other overcome these temptations.

I offer a word of caution here since I've seen a lot of hurt come from not following this simple principle. As you get to know the person during dating or engagement and begin to see his or her flaws, it might be easy to have the attitude that you will change the person. But, before marrying, you must be willing to accept the person for who he or she is, realizing there is no perfect person. You cannot change someone else; only God can. I like what Benjamin Franklin supposedly said, "Before marriage have your eyes wide open and after marriage have them half shut!" Trust God to do the changing.

This intimate, one-flesh relationship also implies teamwork. A close husband and wife learn to work together in all circumstances, whether in prosperous times or times of adversity. Scripture states: "Two are better than one because they have a good return for their labor. For if either of them falls, the one will lift up his companion" (Ecclesiastes 4:9-10). To start preparing for marriage now, you should learn how to work as a teammate with others.

The last verse of Genesis 2 states that no barriers existed between the first husband and wife. "And the man and his wife were both naked and were not ashamed." We now live on the other side of Genesis 2, and all relationships have the elements of shame and fear (which are introduced in Genesis 3), or a myriad of other things that hinder intimacy. Couples now have to continually work at achieving intimacy *because good marriages do not just happen; they are made to happen.* Let's consider two things that help with intimacy.

Learn to Die to Self

There's nothing like self-focus to hinder relationships! Remember, though, that one of the basic principles of Christianity is learning how to be a servant of others. Our Savior was an amazing example of this when he washed the disciples' feet (John 13), and ultimately when he died for our sins. One basic hindrance to having a meaningful relationship is that many times we are not willing to yield to another because we want our own way. Relationships are smoother when people are living for others, and are not living to maintain their own rights. The people who live to defend their rights will have a life of conflict, because they will constantly antagonize others or be antagonized by others. People who learn to serve others will have a more peaceful life. At times in marriage when you realize that your expectations are not being met, consider that these expectations may be selfish, and the answer is to keep your marriage commitment, die to self and love your spouse. Are there ways you could start practicing this perspective now?

Vulnerability

Another element of dying to self is learning to be vulnerable. I have counseled married men who have never learned to confide in others about what they are really thinking or feeling, and this lack of openness hinders their marriages. They retain hurts and emotions that the Lord never intended them to bear, because they have not learned how to cast them upon the Lord nor how to turn to others as a resource to help shoulder life's burdens. The husband-wife relationship as a "one-flesh" relationship was designed by the Lord to be a resource for helping carry life's burdens. Are there ways you could practice being more vulnerable now?

Leaving and Cleaving and Weaving

The last part of God's plan that we need to understand is just how primary and permanent God designed marriage to be. Scripture makes it clear that God's plan is for this union to become the primary human relationship, by the couple leaving father and mother. The word "leave" is a strong Hebrew word translated "forsake" in Psalm 22:1. Our Savior quoted this Psalm when he cried, "My God, My God, why have you forsaken Me?" (Matthew 27:46). In the phrase "cleave to his wife" we also have the principle that marriage is to be a permanent relationship. [42] In this "one-fleshness" the couple then weave their life together.

In looking for a spouse or thinking about one person in particular, ask yourself, "Can I commit to this person as being the primary person in my life for the rest of my life?" Your honest answer can be a test to determine whether or not you are ready for marriage. If you cannot sense a deep and settled commitment, you should not marry that person.

My Friend Eric

My friend "Eric" (that's not his real name) sent me an email that summarizes the pain of separation and divorce. He wrote, "Ernie, I'm looking right at the separation agreement … It's hitting me about like I thought it would … Half of me is ready to start the new life the Lord is giving me, the other half is hating that I have to go through with all this and will come out of it saying that I am divorced … I never thought I'd ever be able to say that … I always pictured that I would get married once and then I'd die … I really need some prayer and encouragement right now … I'm starting to feel the anger inside me … I don't like it but it's hard to fight … Anyway, now more than ever, I could really use a lot of prayer … I've been very lonely … I need some good friends …"

I can feel the grief inside me as I read this again. From knowing both Eric and his wife, I know that they did not understand God's design for marriage and therefore their marriage house was being built on the wrong foundation. Sin has done this to Eric, but I really believe that God in his grace can protect you from this type of pain if you will follow the Architect's blueprint for marriage.

Starting to prepare now:

1.   What do you believe marriage is about? How does your view compare with what you have just read?

2.   Since marriage is about a team reflecting the glory of God, how can you practice being a good teammate with others now?

3.   Which of God's purposes for marriage do you have the most questions about?

4.   What fears do you have about marriage? How does Scripture address those fears?

5.   Write a prayer of commitment to the Lord to follow his purposes for marriage, and decide that you will look only for a spouse who has the same commitments.

Questions to ask about a potential spouse:

1.   Is this person committed to God's purposes for marriage?

2.   Is this person, first of all, your friend?

3.   Does this person seem overly needy?

Part Two
The First Floor

Part One established ways to lay a solid foundation. It's time now to learn how to build the first floor properly.

Part Two explores five key questions:

1. How should I use my single years? (Chapter 5)
2. What relationship skills do I need to develop? (Chapter 6)
3. How do I know when I am ready to be married? (Chapter 7)
4. How will I know God's will? (Chapter 8)
5. What method should I choose to find a spouse? (Chapter 9)

Chapter 5

WISE LIVING DURING
THE SINGLE YEARS

And this I say ... to secure undistracted devotion to the
Lord

1 Corinthians 7:35

When I built homes with my father, I looked forward to the times
when we were finally ready to start putting up the walls of the main
floor. We had done a lot of work before that—getting the foundation poured, constructing solid basement walls, and then putting
down the floor on top of the basement walls. We were now ready to
frame each portion of the main floor walls. We had some exciting
times as we would put together a section and then try to raise it and
get it attached before the wind caught the wall and tried to blow it
out of place.

We have also worked to get the proper foundation in place for
your future marriage house. Now, if you are willing to put in the
time, instead of having a weak relationship built upon the foundation of lustful or shallow desires, you will be more likely to have a
strong relationship built upon wise principles of Scripture. As you
work hard to build, I would remind you that all followers of Christ
are a work in progress. Scripture calls this sanctification. It is the
process of construction in our lives through which the Lord is help-

ing us become more like himself, and this process is as amazing as it sounds (Romans 8:28-29).

Think of this next section as raising the walls of the main floor. Each of the following five chapters will help you construct another section that you will need as you live life preparing for your marriage house, even before being in a relationship. These chapters will answer questions you may have:

1. How should I spend my single years?
2. What relationship skills should I work on while I am single?
3. How will I know when I am ready to be married?
4. How will I know God's will for choosing the right person to marry?
5. What method should I use to find the right spouse?

The Single Years

The construction of the first wall will be solid if we endeavor to carefully answer the question: what does a wise investment of your single years look like? I love working with singles because some of the most important and perplexing questions of life come up during these years. Related questions include: How do I battle sexual temptation? What do I do about loneliness? And, will I ever get married?

Bill

Before I offer some guidance, I would like to tell you about Bill. My conversation with Bill reminds me of how painful these years can be.

One day after our worship service he approached me and asked if we could talk. We had hardly begun our conversation when he started crying. He had been searching for a long time to find the right girl to marry, and the girl whom he was absolutely sure he would marry had just dumped him. His hopes were crushed yet again, and he was feeling loneliness in a fresh way. My heart ached as Bill spoke from the great pain in his soul.

I knew from previous counseling with him that he had recurring problems with relationships. He continually struggled with loving the Lord as his first priority because he was completely convinced that he could never be happy until he was married. It seemed he was so consumed with finding a wife that he was not faithful in his own relationship to the Lord or to our local church. Because he was primarily pursuing marriage instead of the Lord, he would put inappropriate pressure on young ladies, and they would run.

In other words, his whole life was distracted. I actually believe he was squandering much of the potential of his single years, so I counseled Bill to stand on the promise of Matthew 6:33: "But seek first His kingdom and His righteousness; and all these things shall be added to you."

Jeffrey Forrey writes, "Often singles become enveloped in a fog of loneliness and sadness that obscures their vision of their future and of the One who is directing that future by His sovereign decree." [43] I know Bill felt this way, and maybe you do too. In these years of uncertainty and struggle, you may experience the loneliness, perplexity and isolation that these times can bring, but you have the perfect solution for problems—God's Word, the Holy Spirit in your life, and your brothers and sisters in Christ! I've often thought how applicable Psalm 27:13-14 is for singles," I would have despaired unless I had believed that I would see the goodness of the LORD in the land of the living; wait for the LORD; take courage; yes, wait for the LORD."

1 Corinthians 7

A key chapter to address many of these issues is 1 Corinthians 7. This chapter addresses questions that the church at Corinth had sent to Paul. They lived in a sexually promiscuous culture (like many around the world today), so their questions may have revolved around the sexual relationship within marriage. Some may have asked, "Paul, isn't it more spiritual to remain single?" "Paul, how do I know if I am to remain single and serve the Lord as a single?" "Paul, because our city is so centered on sexuality, wouldn't it be more spiritual to refrain from a sexual relationship with my spouse just to show a deeper relationship with Christ?" He answered by saying things like, "But because of immoralities, let each man have his own wife, and let each woman have her own husband" (verse 2). And, "Yet I wish that all men were even as I myself am [i.e., single]. However each has his own gift from God.... But I say to the unmarried and the widows that it is good for them if they remain even as I. But if they do not have self-control, let them marry; for it is better to marry than to burn" (verses 7-9).

I know it might be uncomfortable to consider, but these verses naturally bring up the question of the *gift* of singleness, that is, remaining single to use your life for Christ. This idea may sound strange, but it is worthwhile because it forces you to deal with issues that you might not otherwise address, including having a realistic picture of married life. Understanding Paul's reasoning in this chapter can help you discern whether you are called to be single or to be married. And, if you are called to be married, you can be reassured because you'll realize that's how the Lord designed you.

Let's think about this in more detail. Practically speaking, Paul meant that you should choose to remain single only if you have the *gift* of singleness. He probably considered this a spiritual gift, just as there are other gifts given to the church. [44] These "spiritual gifts" are listed in a number of places in the New Testament, including just a few chapters later (chapter 12). If you really have this gift, it would allow you to devote yourself fully to ministry instead of adding the responsibilities of marriage.

Stephen Vantassel puts it well. He is speaking about those with the gift of singleness, but I believe all can have this attitude during their single years as they wait for the Lord's will to be worked out.

> Celibate people use their freedom for God's work, not for personal gratification. Celibacy is a choice of the single life for service to Christ, not from an inordinate desire to flee responsibility and commitment. Celibacy is a gift to free you to use another gift to serve others. Celibacy is not an end to itself.... Celibacy should require an individual to use the time that would have been spent

meeting the needs of spouse and children in meeting the needs of the church. [45]

If you determine that you do have the gift of singleness, it does not make you holier than those who marry. In other words, Paul did not encourage singleness to the detriment of marriage. We know this from Ephesians 5 where Paul wrote some of the most well-known verses on marriage, and recognizes its high place in God's plans because it represents Christ's relationship with his church. Also, just a few chapters after his discussion on singleness he writes, "Do we not have a right to take along a believing wife, even as the rest of the apostles, and the brothers of the Lord, and Cephas?" (1 Corinthians 9:5). He simply emphasizes that, especially in the "present distress," those with the gift of singleness should make the most of it.

Paul was concerned because of some type of distressful situation the Christians were about to face. He says, "I think then that this is good in view of the present distress that it is good for a man to remain as he is" (1 Corinthians 9:26). Paul may write from the perspective that the Lord would soon return, or he may have sensed that persecution was about to break out against Christians. Whatever the situation, it prompted Paul to urge them to live as if "the time has been shortened" (verse 29).

In 1 Corinthians 7:35 Paul captures his desire for all of the people in the church at Corinth. "And this I say ... to secure undistracted devotion to the Lord." I know a lot of people who need to hear this same advice today. His desire was for them to have a focused commitment to the Lord whether they remain single or get married.

We're about to look at some questions that can help you determine if you might have this gift of singleness, but first, let's look at some examples of those who had this gift. Has it ever occurred to you that the two most influential people in the New Testament were single? Both Paul and our Lord were not married. We also have the example of Anna in Luke 2:36-38,

> And there was a prophetess, Anna … She was advanced in years, having lived with a husband seven years after her marriage, and then as a widow to the age of eighty-four. Anna never left the temple, serving night and day with fasting and prayers.

Isn't it amazing to think that for decades she had dedicated herself exclusively to the service of the Lord? Think of the ministry impact of using your life in this way.

These examples demonstrate abundantly that you can be a complete man or woman without being married. At least we'd better say that. The alternative is to say that our Lord was not a complete man by being single, but that would be heresy!

Matthew 19:12 also mentions how some choose to remain single. "There are also eunuchs who made themselves eunuchs for the sake of the kingdom of heaven." Based upon 1 Corinthians 7, this verse, and the teaching of Scripture on marriage, it would be good to pose some questions to help determine if you have the gift of singleness. Please consider these:

> Do I desire to be free to focus solely on the Lord and his work?
>
> Do I often think about having my own family?
>
> Does the thought of not having a family cause me a sense of
>
> grief or loss?
>
> Do I have a problem with sexual self-control?
>
> Do I want the responsibilities of being a spouse and parent?

What is your giftedness?

Perhaps as you answer these questions, you realize that you do not have the gift of singleness, and for many of you that's a big relief. Even if you do not have this gift, it doesn't mean you have no giftedness. God gives spiritual gifts to each person who becomes a Christian (1 Corinthians 12:7). These gifts include among other things, service, teaching, exhortation, giving, administration, and mercy. Whatever your giftedness, I hope you will realize it and use it for the Lord. Sadly, I've met many older people who have never understood what the Lord has gifted them to do, and that has led to a lack of effectiveness in serving him. Please look at the list in Romans 12 and ask yourself what the Lord has designed you to do in his church. Also, you might think of godly people who know you well and seek their counsel.

You may be really busy now, but add to your life a spouse and some children, soccer games, school meetings, and helping with homework, and you can readily see that a married person is probably even busier. I know it's hard to believe. But the point is, while you have the opportunity, dedicate yourself to using your giftedness in order to make an impact for Christ.

The Priority of the Local Church

I hope you do ask, "How can I use my single years to make an impact for the Lord?" I urge you to begin in your local church. Join the choir, work in the children's ministry, visit those in the hospital or in nursing homes, get involved with discipleship, or offer to do childcare for the pastor and his wife so they can have some time out. These activities also help combat the loneliness you may feel as a single.

While serving in your local church, you will get to meet others who truly love the Lord, and you will begin to figure out some of the gifts he has given you. Who knows, your future spouse may be involved in the same ministry. Putting it bluntly, do you think that God will bless you with a spouse if you are willing to serve him faithfully during your single years? The biblical advice I gave Bill applies to you as well, "But seek first his kingdom and His righteousness; and all these things shall be added to you" (Matthew 6:33).

There are, of course, other places for ministry, but I would urge you to consider your local church first. I know this is hard, especially if you are involved with one of the many excellent campus ministries that are available and needed. But I emphasize this because the local church is neglected today. It is my conviction that God intends to use not just "the church" in general to reach the world, but the local church in particular. Have you ever considered that the letters written by many New Testament writers were written to a local church, not just "the church?" God desires to work through your local church, with all its members using their gifts to minister to the world (see 1 Corinthians 12 and Romans 12).

Paul provides a clear example of loyalty and accountability to his local church. In Acts 13:1-2 we see that his church (at Antioch) sent him out on his missionary journeys, and then when he returns two chapters later, he goes immediately back to his local church to report. Many believers today, however, do not practice this type of commitment to their church. I would urge you to discover both the joys of using your gifts in your own church and the depth of relationships that can be developed.

Joey

In a church where I was pastor we had a wonderful example of a young man who had the right attitude about his single years. Joey attended church regularly, ministered to others and discipled others. He, and others, visited and helped widows. They even built relationships with boys from a disadvantaged neighborhood in order to lead them to the gospel. All the while, they attended college and were excellent students. While I clearly understand that you can become overcommitted, when your life is busy it forces you to use your time more wisely. I believe this is what happened with Joey. Because he was trying to stay focused primarily on the Lord (unlike Bill who was obsessed with finding a wife), he was attracted to young ladies who were also motivated to serve the Lord. He desired a relationship based on honoring Christ. I encouraged Joey to remember this verse from Psalm 37: 7, "Delight yourself in the Lord and He will give you the desires of your heart." The Lord did honor his faithfulness and provided him with a godly wife.

A Strategy for Sexual Temptation

It is also obvious from 1 Corinthians 7 that sexual temptations do create a major challenge. Paul states it clearly, almost graphically, in verse 9, "… It is better to marry than to burn." But if marriage isn't on the immediate horizon, how do you handle the burning desires? Because I regularly counsel those who are struggling with sexual temptation, I know it can be a very difficult and frustrating battle.

I am certain that you can experience growth as you practice principles taught in Scripture. In 1 Corinthians 9, Paul compares the ability to exercise self-control with the dedication of an athlete training for an event. You have to be highly motivated and passionate about your sport. You train rigorously and constantly as you strive for the prize. What will motivate you to exercise such self-control? Two things helped Paul to deny himself—love for God and for others. He said, "I discipline my body and make it my slave" (1 Corinthians 9:27). If you look a few verses above this one, you see that his motivation for self-control was other people and the gospel. In other words, he wanted to show love for the Lord, and love for others so they would be lead to become followers of Jesus.

Just as we saw in chapter 3 when we discussed loving God and loving others, love is a powerful weapon in our arsenal to attack temptation. For example, when sexual temptation comes, ask, "What would be the most loving thing to do for my future spouse?" You can show love for your future spouse by keeping yourself pure now. Unfortunately, your memory will not be erased the moment you get married. If you are not diligent or wise now, you will carry memories into your marriage of sexual experiences when you were single. That's not fair to your future husband or wife.

A man told me how powerful this principle has been in his life. He had struggled with sexual temptation for a long time. He became interested in a certain young lady, and they both believed the Lord was leading them toward marriage. When he was tempted sexually, he began rehearsing in his mind this principle of loving his future wife more than the desire he had. It helped him to exercise self-control and to gain the victory over the temptation. At that moment he was like an athlete denying himself some pleasure for the sake of the team and for the sake of winning the prize. The prize here would be more stability, contentment, and intimacy with your future spouse. The reward will be a clear conscience and less guilt.

Your love for the Lord becomes your strongest weapon against sexual temptation and, even better, for changing your desires. You can see impure sexual longings subside as you derive more pleasure from your relationship with the Lord than from giving in to the temptations. As your awe for and trust in the Lord grow, your ability to say no to lesser "loves" is greater. There are such things as superior pleasures and loves and inferior pleasures and loves, just as there are legitimate pleasures and illegitimate pleasures. Edward Welch states it well: "As Jesus is known and exalted among us, you will notice that self-control becomes more obvious." [46]

And,

> Scripture does not oppose strong desire; instead, it approves of it and commands it. The problem is in the purpose of our passions. Do our passions express a heart that seeks the glory of Christ and intensely desires the things which Jesus desires? Or do they express our own desires to serve ourselves and our own glory? It is likely that part of the repentance of addictions should include repentance for not being passionate about—lusting enough after—Christ and the things that He loves. [47]

To experience increasing successes over sexual temptation ask, "What do I love more?" "Do I love the Lord, others, and my future spouse more than I love this area of temptation?" We reveal our selfishness when we choose our intense desires over loving God and others. Short-sightedness is also revealed when we give in to immediate gratification rather than consider long-term, more satisfying gratification. Unfortunately, we often give in to our desires. The answer is to ask forgiveness of the Lord and endeavor again to grow in love. His grace is amazing and reassuring when shame tries to dominate our souls. We can remind ourselves, "There is … no condemnation for those who are in Christ Jesus" (Rom. 8:1). And, he forgave "… us all our transgressions, having cancelled out the certificate of debt … against us and which was hostile to us; and He has taken it out of the way, having nailed it to the cross" (Col. 2:13-14). Be encouraged, it's never too late to start doing what's right.

This raises the significant question: since a superior love for and delight in the Lord will defeat an inferior delight in illegitimate sexual pleasure, how do I grow in love for the Lord? The answer is that you grow in love for him just as you grow in love for others. We love another because of his or her characteristics, that is, who he or she is as a person.

We also love him or her because of attractiveness. So, applying this to the Lord—meditate on his beauty. Because you can't actually see him, how do you do this? I believe that's one of the roles of creation. Just as artwork shows what an artist is like, creation shows what the Creator must be like. If a sunset catches your eye, then turn it into worship. If a flower garden is beautiful, then imagine how much more beautiful the Creator must be!

You can grow in your love by thinking about the depth of his sacrifice for you on the cross. What amazing love! If your relationship with the Lord seems blah then you probably haven't had a fresh look at the cross recently. How about reading one of the crucifixion accounts while asking the Lord to take off your blinders and give you a new look at the cross. Or, think about some of the many attributes of God—his mercy, grace, forgiveness, eternality, and be in awe that this all powerful God desires a relationship with you. How can you not love One so wonderful?

You Don't Need Sex

Another weapon in your arsenal to fight sexual temptation is to realize that you don't need premarital sex. It seems that everything in your body tells you otherwise, and so does the culture. Sex sells cars, clothes, Coke, and many other products. John Piper makes the point succinctly,

> The most fully human person who has ever lived, or ever will live, is Jesus Christ, and He never once had sexual intercourse.... We will always have mountains of truly human Christ-likeness yet to climb, but sexual intercourse is not one of them. For He never knew it. And He is infinitely whole. [48]

American culture (like many cultures) makes so much of sex because sex is an idol. People look for true joy in an intimate sexual encounter, but if they are honest, they find out that it does not deliver its promise. It is a wonderful gift of God, but sex in itself cannot offer deep fulfillment.

A Proper Mindset Toward the Opposite Sex

To deal with sexual temptation properly, you need a new attitude toward the opposite sex. Paul is not naive about sexual temptation when he commands Timothy, "Do not sharply rebuke an older man, but rather appeal to him as a father, to the younger men as brothers, the older women as mothers, *and the younger women as sisters, in all purity* [emphasis mine] (1 Timothy 5: 2). Timothy is to treat the younger women of the church "with all purity." Instead of having wrong desires for the young women, he should desire to protect them like a big brother. Treat the young women in your life accordingly. How would you treat your sister? How would you look at your sister?

Having lived in a university town convinced me that many girls can be naïve about the way guys' minds work (I know some aren't). Ladies, you must think through modesty issues. I deal with enough men to know that the way a girl dresses (or more accurately, does not dress) causes lust problems for men. While men must learn to control their eyes and thoughts, you too must show self-control in your manner of dress. You can practice loving your brothers in Christ by dressing modestly. Most men struggle with temptation when they see women wearing tight or revealing clothes. In general, the tighter the clothes and the more skin revealed, the greater the temptation. A principle for you to consider is, "what I attract them with I attract them to." If you have not been taught how to be modest, go to a godly older woman in your church for advice. Ladies, ask yourself, "Am I trying to attract men with my body?" The world encourages this attitude, but it should not be the attitude of a Christian woman.

Developing a Realistic View of Sex

Many couples enter marriage with a naïve view of marriage. Instead of putting marriage on a pedestal, you need a healthy dose of reality. You need to understand some of the obligations that Paul says married couples will have. "Let the husband fulfill his duty to his wife, and likewise also the wife to her husband. The wife does not have authority over her body, but the husband does; likewise also the husband does not have authority over his own body, but the wife does" (1 Corinthians 7:3-4). Paul had to remind men and women of their sexual obligations in marriage because some were proposing that abstinence was more spiritual.

You may come from a home where no one talked to you about a proper sexual relationship. As a result, you can enter marriage without understanding the sexual obligations that you have. Ladies, you may not have fully dealt with the fact that when you get married, "the wife does not have authority over her own body, but the husband does." This does not mean that a husband can mistreat nor abuse you, because that would violate many other biblical principles. It does mean that you, as a wife, may need to realize that a passionate sexual relationship with your husband is good and right. Just read the Song of Solomon! Men you must realize that God's Word tells you, "Husbands ought also to love their own wives as their own bodies " (Ephesians 5:28a). "Let marriage be held in honor among all, and let the marriage bed be undefiled" (Hebrews 13:4a).

The problem may be just the opposite though by placing higher expectations on the sexual relationship. Many couples think that a more satisfying sexual relationship will solve all of their problems, and then marriage will be great. I have counseled enough married couples to know that simply having regular physical intimacy does not fix all unresolved issues.

Marriage Is Temporary

You need to remember that marriage is for this life only. I still remember writing "Ernie and Rose Forever," but as nice as it sounds, it's just not true. Scripture shows us that marriage is an earthly picture of Christ's relationship with his church. Paul states clearly in 1 Corinthians 7:34, "one who is married is concerned about the things of the world, how she may please her husband." He had just told them "the form of this world is passing away" (7:31). In other words, marriage is part of the form of this world that is passing away. The contrast is between a single person being able to devote himself to the things of the Lord and the person who is married not being able to fully concentrate on ministry because he has marriage obligations. I know that takes some of the romantic feelings out of our dreams of marriage, but with our society's 50 percent divorce rate, doesn't it seem that we need to think realistically about marriage?

Another reality that Paul teaches is that a husband must care for the needs of his wife, and the wife for the needs of her husband (verses 33-34). As a Christian you cannot neglect the needs of your spouse or of the children that the Lord gives you. They need a home, food, clothes, and loving attention. Bills will need to be paid, lawns mowed, and dishes washed. There will be a lot more on your mind than being passionate with your spouse! I hope that during your single years you will ask the Lord to help you develop a realistic view of marriage.

Research shows that young people are searching for a "soul mate," the one person who can perfectly meet all their needs. This dangerous trend amplifies unrealistic expectations. The National Marriage Project stated,

> The findings in this survey suggest that today's young adults may be reaching even higher in their expectations for marriage. The centuries old ideal of friendship in marriage, or what sociologists call companionate marriage, may be evolving into a more exalted and demanding standard of a spiritualized union of souls. [49]

Putting it bluntly, there are no perfect marriages. There is not a perfect spouse. All humans have flaws, and you will not find your perfect need-meeter in a spouse. The original sin of Genesis 3 has tainted everything. This implies that you will be disappointed with your spouse. You will feel anger. You will have to forgive. This is the reality of life in a fallen world filled with fallen people. Yet it is exciting to see the gospel lived out in relationships, and it is also reassuring to see that biblical principles work!

Singleness and Money

In an age of consumer debt, increasing college tuition, and student loans, it is important to address some biblical principles related to money. It is wonderful to realize yet again that the Lord has not left us without guidance. A key principle is found in Psalm 24:1-2, "The earth is the LORD's, and all it contains, the world and those who dwell in it. For He has founded it upon the seas and established it upon the rivers." Yet another is, Matthew 6:21 and 24 where the Lord says, "Where your treasure is, there your heart will be also…. You cannot serve God and mammon."

Psalm 24 confronts us with who really owns everything and why he can claim it, and Matthew 6, like laser surgery, pinpoints the true source of the problem with money and possessions. The Lord teaches us that our treasures truly reveal our hearts.

One of the many implications is that you need to know your heart, and again I'm speaking of the heart here as I did in chapter 3. To help you discern what is happening in your heart concerning money, you can ask yourself the following questions: How much do money and material things tempt your inner person to worship the wrong things? To what degree do you think that buying things will make you happy?

Some of you may have grown up in homes where everything was provided for you and you had many possessions. Some of you though may have been raised in a home where it always seemed like money was tight and you had few possessions. It is equally easy for either the rich or poor person to think that having more money or possessions is the answer to life.

It is vitally important for your preparation for life and marriage that you begin to learn how to be wise with money. So, here are some more questions to help you think about areas that may need to be addressed. Are you learning the discipline and joy of supporting your local church financially? To what degree can you say no to your desires to buy new things? Have you begun to establish guidelines for how your weekly income is spent? And it might be worth considering that, as you learn to exhibit self-control with money, you will be demonstrating to your parents that you have grown to be more prepared for life and marriage.

Encouragement

If you find yourself despairing, feeling lonely and wondering when marriage might happen, I would remind you again to meditate on, and choose to believe, Psalm 27, especially verses 13 and 14. "I would have despaired unless I had believed that I would see the goodness of the LORD in the land of the living. Wait for the LORD; be strong and let your heart take courage; yes, wait for the LORD." His timing is perfect, and he does have a wonderful plan for your life. In the meantime, I hope you will determine to use your single years wisely.

Starting to prepare now:

1. Are you involved in using your gifts in a local church? If not, how could you start?

2. Do you know what your spiritual gift is? What are you passionate about?

3. Read 1Corinthians 12, and Romans 12:1-8.

4. Which of the principles discussed do you need to put into practice regarding sexual purity?

5. In what areas do you suspect that you have an unrealistic view of marriage?

6. How can you grow in your discipline toward finances and attitude toward material things?

7. Write a prayer of commitment concerning how you want to use your single years.

Questions to ask about a potential spouse:

1. Is this person committed to the local church, and how is he or she using giftedness?

2. How is sexual purity demonstrated in this person's life?

3. What amount of school loans and other debt does this person have?

Chapter 6

THE INGREDIENTS OF WISE RELATIONSHIPS

(Relationship Skills and Character Traits)

> Walk in a manner worthy of the calling with which
> you have been called, with all humility and gentleness,
> with all patience, showing forbearance to one another
> in love.
>
> Ephesians 4:1b-2

Liz and John

Liz and John had been married for less than a year when they came to me for help. All married couples experience adjustments during the first year of marriage, but not as many as these two! Married life had become a nightmare for both of them, and they acted as if they hated each other.

Both were graduate students, and they both had heavy demands on their time. Liz took her schoolwork very seriously, and she admitted that she put more emphasis on her research than she did on her marriage. Although he was gifted academically, John was satisfied with B's instead of A's, and he admitted that playing with their money through online investments had become more than a hobby. Whenever he wanted to watch television or spend time online, she would accuse him of being irresponsible. He would accuse her of loving school more than she loved him. The tension had escalated until they would yell at each other and even lock each other out of the apartment. Things became particularly ugly when one was in the hall trying to push the door open as the other was inside trying to keep the door closed, and the neighbors began to ask questions. The Lord used this incident to get their attention. Help was needed and right away.

When they came to me they were both very ashamed about how their marriage had degenerated so quickly. I was thankful both were teachable. It brought me joy to have them accept counsel from Scripture that helped them understand why they were acting as they were and how they could strengthen their marriage. It was obvious that they needed to work on relationship skills, like honoring one another and improving their communication, but they also needed to understand what was motivating them in the depths of their inner persons. They were truly living out their selfish desires (see James 4:1-2).

It was true that neither of them had good role models at home; they had never observed or been taught how to practice good relationship skills. During one counseling session I learned that Liz's parents were divorcing. Liz had never been taught how to be a godly wife. John's parents also had a miserable marriage. Except when he was fighting with Liz, John was quiet. On top of that, he had a terrible relationship with his father, so he had no model for becoming a godly husband. They quickly learned that more was going on in their hearts than how each of their families had shaped them (as significant as that was). I was thankful to the Lord that during our meetings they accepted that their active inner persons were interpreting and shaping the way they responded to the other. It was obvious to them that our Lord was correct when he said, "For the mouth speaks out of that which fills the heart" (Matthew 12:34). As you can see, there were a lot of dynamics going on in the relationship. In almost every way imaginable they were weak in knowing how to relate to each other.

We All Need Help

The same is true for many of us. Who we are as people, with our life experiences, personalities, and character traits (all being influenced by our hearts), shapes the way we interact with others. Because of all these ingredients, relationships will be messy and require hard work. Add to this that our hearts are inherently permeated by what happened in Genesis 3, and it is easy to see why we have a default tendency to respond sinfully in relationships. We can be too harsh or too soft, too aggressive or too lenient, and often with the people we say we love the most. Ironic, but true.

Furthermore, we must put regular effort into relationships because things in this fallen world tend toward depletion and disorganization. Just as your house needs regular maintenance because things deteriorate, so do relationships. Ignore maintenance on your room for a while and see what happens! Because these things are self-evidently true, we must learn now what it takes to have healthy relationships. You should not wait until you are married and hope that magically you'll be a relational wizard.

Good relationship skills and character traits should become second nature to you so that you never create the distressing situations that Liz and John had experienced during their first year of marriage. All this takes time. It takes time to learn the character traits and skills that make strong relationships. A few sessions of premarital counseling right before marriage cannot teach you all that you need to know, much less give you time to work these principles into your life.

There's plenty to work on now. In this chapter we'll consider the character and relationship skills you can use with others, who you are as a person, and what you are able to do.

Proper Motivations

Let's think first about the proper motivations for working on these things. Without proper inner motivations for developing relationships, you may become an expert at development but may also use relationship skills to manipulate others. Business management experts emphasize that if you want to change something, begin with focus groups to make people think that their opinion is important so that you can get your agenda through. Others recommend learning "how to win friends and influence people" so that you can increase your business profits. Leaders are taught how to "stroke" people and give them what they want in order to increase their output. We must be careful that our people skills come from proper heart motivations.

What would be correct motivations for relationship skills? The New Testament regularly emphasizes the importance of having good relationships. We are commanded to practice the "one anothers," with the main theme being to "love one another" (John 13:34-35; 15:12). It is interesting that the main author of the New Testament often wrote about Christian relationships. Ephesians 4:1-6 and Colossians 3:1-4:1 are excellent examples of this. But in these books Paul especially discusses the motivations for working on relationships with one another. In these passages he gives doctrinal reasons for good relationship skills before giving practical commands. His point is that our doctrine (what we believe) affects the way we live.

Paul emphasizes that one motivation for developing healthy character traits and practicing relationship skills is that we must realize that we are a part of the body of Christ, and we should want to be more Christlike.

Being Related to Christ

Let's look more closely at Ephesians 4. Paul's theme for this book is "Jesus Christ is the Head of his Body, the Church." He explains in the first three chapters that believers in Jesus Christ are part of this amazing group called the church. In Ephesians 2:8-10 he says that we became part of this not by our own works but by grace through faith. We have been given this relationship with Christ so that as the Lord works in our lives, we will produce evidence of this relationship. In other words, the church is saved to display certain things God considers important. He then changes us so that these "good works" are accomplished in our lives. What good works does God consider important?

Remember that Paul typically divided his writing between what we believe and how we live because of what we believe. In Ephesians this divides nicely between chapters 1-3 and 4-6. So, the "good works" section, where he explains how we should be living, starts with chapter 4, and relationship character traits and skills are right at the top of the list

Relationships are Top Priority

When Paul begins discussing how this doctrine affects our lives, he addresses relationship character traits right away. He says that this is the way we live up to what we claim to be part of—the church, the body of Christ. Maybe when you think of good works, you think of caring for the poor or faithfully worshiping or reading your Bible. It is really significant that out of all the different areas he could have chosen to demonstrate that our beliefs affect our behavior, Paul starts with relationships.

He challenges us to live up to our calling and then states that those who do will be "diligent to preserve the unity of the Spirit in the bond of peace" (Eph. 4:3). He also tells us to be patient and bear with one another (4:2).

So, our first motivation for learning and practicing Christlike character traits and relationship skills is that we are part of something bigger, the body of Christ. These qualities are to be the natural attitudes and behaviors of those being transformed by the gospel. Isn't it interesting that relationships rank highest on Paul's list of things that illustrate that the church is the body of Christ?

In Paul's mind, holy living always happens in association with others. This theme is so significant in Ephesians that almost every application Paul gives in chapters 4 through 6 recognizes that if Christ is the head of your life, this affects your relationships. Christianity is about the group, and the world needs to see something radically different in the way we deal with one another. How can we have an impact on the world if we treat one another in the same way that unsaved people treat one another? How can a Christian couple claim that Christ is making a difference in their lives if they fight in the same way the world does? Chapter 1 tells us that because we have been graciously forgiven, then we ought to graciously forgive others. If we have been shown abundant mercy, then we ought to be abundantly merciful.

Those who are being transformed by Christ, are recognized by their character traits. "By this the children of God and the children of the devil are obvious: anyone who does not practice righteousness is not of God, nor the one who does not love his brother. For this is the message which you have heard from the beginning, that we should love one another" (1 John 3:10-11).

Our Powerful Model

Many of you may have grown up in homes where there was no model of patience or sacrificial love or other character traits that make a home enjoyable. Wouldn't it be helpful to have a perfect example of how to develop relationships? We do! The Lord gives us his own example to show what these characteristics are like.

Think about how much relationships matter to the Lord. The gospel is about the Lord tearing down the barriers that stood between our Creator and fallen humanity. He sent his Son to die for our sin so that we can be reconciled to him. Also, he broke down the barrier between Jew and Gentile so that a new group of people called the church could be created (Ephesians 2:11-18). He goes to great lengths to see relationships restored! So should we.

Our Savior also modeled these wonderful character traits. He was kind and patient and cared deeply for others. Men, we are notorious for poor relationship skills, and we can use the excuse that "it's just the way men are" to avoid learning how to relate well to others. Yet Jesus, the perfect man, was perfect in the character traits that enhance relationships and perfect in relationship skills. He is our model of the perfect *gentleman.*

Specific Character Traits

Just as in Ephesians 4, Colossians 3: 12-14 lists character qualities that enhance relationships. [50] The theme of Colossians is similar to that of Ephesians—Christ is the hero. When our Savior is the preeminent one in our lives, his character qualities will start to be manifested in our lives. Let's combine the lists of character traits from these two passages to understand how our Lord impacts our character and how these traits influence our relationships.

1. Heart of Compassion:[51] The word heart was used to describe the viscera, the vital organs deep inside the body. The word compassion is also translated as mercy. Putting both together then, we are called to have deep feelings of mercy for one another. Mercy starts on the inside and results in acts of compassion. You will find yourself "weeping with those who weep and rejoicing with those who rejoice" (Romans 12:15). All of these character traits are modeled by our Lord. For example, "Blessed be the God and Father of our Lord Jesus Christ, the Father of mercies and God of all comfort" (2 Corinthians 1:3). Have you begun to show a "heart of compassion" for others in your life?

2. Kindness: This word illustrates the point that character qualities begin on the inside as attitudes and are expressed in actions. The word can be translated "kindness," "goodness of heart" or even "uprightness." If you have a kind attitude, it will be shown in kind actions. If you develop kindness in your life, it will be a characteristic that strengthens your marriage house, glorifies God, and makes it easier for others to love you.

Again, God is the model, "Or do you think lightly of the riches of His kindness and forbearance and patience, not knowing that the kindness of God leads you to repentance" (Romans 2:4). Two times in this verse our God is described as kind. We are told we shouldn't take God's kindness lightly. It is only because he is kind that we are not immediately judged and that anyone comes to know Jesus as his or her Savior. He holds back what we deserve (in mercy) and gives us what we do not deserve (in grace). How are you doing with holding back on what others deserve and giving them what they don't deserve?

These first two characteristics can be summarized by one Old Testament term used as a chief characteristic of God, "lovingkindness" (see Psalm 36:5 as an example). The Hebrew word is so rich that a single English word can't capture God's heart of compassion combined with kindness. When you compare this with God's wrath, you realize that it takes a lot to stir up his anger, but he pours out his lovingkindness quite easily.

3. **Humility**: This word literally means "low mindedness." Our Lord is our example because he was so humble that he was willing to die on the cross for us (Philippians 2:1-11). Pride or self-centeredness destroys relationships, but humility enhances them. The humble person will be willing to listen to others and to serve them. Pride is such a serious problem that Peter wrote, "Clothe yourselves with humility toward one another, for God is opposed to the proud, but gives grace to the humble" (1 Peter 5:5). It will be easier for others to love you if you willingly put them first and sacrifice for them.

4. **Gentleness**: This word is often translated as "meekness," but some people confuse that definition with that of "weakness." It does not mean "weakness" because it is a characteristic of our Lord, and he certainly was never weak. Gentleness is such an important quality that it is described in James 3:16 as that of the truly wise. It is fruit of the Spirit for all believers (Galatians 5:3), and all believers are told to practice this toward all men. Titus 3:2 tells us to be "peaceable, gentle, showing every consideration to all men."

5. **Patience**: The importance of patience is stated in Ephesians 4:1-2: "Walk in a manner worthy of the calling with which you have been called, with all humility and gentleness, with patience showing tolerance for one another in love." Patience is an important characteristic in marriage, especially when children are involved. A home can be a wonderful place when patience is practiced. One of the secrets of learning patience is believing that God is in control of all things. As you choose to trust him, you become more content and as a result more patient.

6. **Bearing with one another:** Bearing with one another might also be called toleration. Even though many cultures abuse this word there

is a proper type of toleration. Bearing with each other is a necessity in relationships because when conflict arises you must be willing to understand the feelings and thoughts of others. It is easy to be impatient and intolerant or have what I call, " big toes." Some people seem to have their feelings hurt by others easily; in other words, it's not hard to step on their toes. By growing in Christlikeness, shouldn't our toes shrink? The more we grow in grace, the more gracious our attitude should be toward others.

7. **Forgiveness**: It is interesting that Paul gives a more comprehensive explanation for this characteristic than he does any of the others. He says, "Forgiving each other, whoever has a complaint against anyone, just as the Lord forgave you, so also should you" (Colossians 3:13). Forgiveness means to grant a favor or a pardon, although it is undeserved, following the example of how our Lord treats us. Forgiveness also means "to send things away" indicating that it is a decision you must make based upon how the Lord has treated you. It is not a feeling. If you wait to feel right about forgiving someone who has harmed you, you probably never will forgive.

It is guaranteed that in your marriage your spouse will do things that will hurt your feelings. Rather than allow resentment to build, you must choose to forgive and overlook. If you allow the Lord to build a forgiving spirit into your heart, your marriage will be more stable. [52] John MacArthur wrote, "Every believer must seek to manifest the forgiving spirit of Joseph (Genesis 50:19-21) and of Stephen (Acts 7:60) as often as needed (Luke 17:3-4). To receive pardon from the perfectly holy God and then to refuse to pardon others when we are sinful men is the epitome of abuse of mercy." [53]

8. **Love**: Paul says that love is "the perfect bond of unity." If love is the glue that holds relationships together, don't you think we ought to understand what this type of love is? Scripture makes it clear that it is a sacrificial love based on commitment. This love shows that you are willing to sacrifice your own desires for others. It is not primarily feeling oriented. God loved us so much that he sacrificed his Son.

Jesus loved us so much that he gave himself for us. "Home is where each lives for the other and all live for God" is a motto that makes family life enjoyable.

After seeing the definitions of these character traits, it is easy to see why John and Liz were failing miserably. They were demonstrating the characteristics that Paul said we must get rid of as children of God, "anger, wrath, malice, slander, and abusive speech" (Colossians 3:8). When you think of a miserable family, it is a home characterized by anger and abusive words instead of peace and joy. It is actually a home that practices the opposite of each of the character traits listed. Go through the list and think of the opposites of these character traits and soon you will see why so many homes are falling apart or in serious need of repair. How about you? Which character trait do you need to work on first? I guarantee that if you work on it your relationships with others will be stronger.

Be Careful of Excuses

It would be easy at this point to think, "I'm just not a gentle person." "That's not the way I am, and others just need to accept that." "It's not my personality." But, if you believe that your personality is unchangeable, then you can never grow to be more like your Savior. Let me give you some good news. You're not stuck! Even though there are aspects of your personality that will always be present, you can still grow to be more patient, loving and gentle, and it is important to see how.

Relationship Skills

Just as certain character qualities enhance relationships, there are also relationship skills that strengthen relationships. Character qualities are *inner person* qualities that work out in actions. Relationship skills are things you *do* with others to strengthen relationships. Character qualities are primarily about *being*. Relationship skills are about *doing*. Both are necessary for healthy relationships.

Literature about what makes healthy relationships frequently emphasizes six specific skills:

- Communication skills—staying up-to-date with one another and just talking about life together
- Conflict resolution skills—knowing how to bring conflicts to resolution
- Understanding roles—knowing who does what and why in the relationship
- Worship—common religious beliefs, heading the same direction spiritually and walking with the Lord together
- Time together—investing in the relationship through time spent
- Honoring and serving one another—doing loving things for each other with an attitude of respect

Emphasizing Communication and Conflict Resolution

It is interesting to me that Paul recognizes the importance of many of these in Ephesians 4 and in the parallel passage in Colossians 3. These skills strengthen relationships at church, at work, and especially at home. Even though there are six, I am going to emphasize two that seem to be most necessary and have many practical ways to be worked on even while you are single. You may have guessed them—communication and conflict resolution.

Communicating Truthfully[54]

It's impossible to have gospel-centered relationships without communicating truthfully with others. Paul writes, "Therefore, laying aside falsehood, speak truth, each of you, with his neighbor, for we are members of one another" (Ephesians 4:25). With each one of the following communication principles, he tells us something that is to be put off because of who we already are in Christ. He also tells us attitudes and behavior to put on and a motivation for doing so.

He begins by emphasizing how important speaking truthfully is for a follower of Christ. Remember that our Lord said that he is the way, the *truth* and the life (John 14:6). Paul wants us to know how serious it is to be dishonest with one another, since we belong to the same body.

It's not surprising that in Ephesians 4:15 Paul emphasized that love must be our motivation for speaking truth. "But speaking the truth in love, we are to grow up in all aspects into Him, who is the head, even Christ." The truth Paul speaks of here is the gospel, but in this context it's about how the gospel is to influence our relationships.

Before you speak, especially about something that could potentially be hurtful, it is wise to ask yourself questions like, "Why do I believe that I need to talk with them about this? What do they need to hear? How are they going to receive this? Are my motives pleasing to the Lord?"

Just think of how important it is to have both truth and love. For example, think of a person who speaks truth, but doesn't do it in love. How does he or she come across? That's right; truth without love comes across harshly. On the other hand, being kind but being afraid to say hard things can be perceived as being weak and unclear. We need both truth and love for effective communication.

A key to honest communication is accurate communication. Think about this. Exaggeration is in the same category as lying. Did that get your attention? It is easy in the heat of an argument to say, "You always ..." or "You never...." Is that actually true? They *never*? These kinds of statements only intensify arguments and break down communication.

Another common violation of this verse is to answer "nothing" when asked, "What is wrong?" You should be truthful in answering. Usually, husbands and wives are guilty of this because they do not want to talk about the issues. It would be better to tell the truth "Yes, there is something wrong," but perhaps ask for time to think about how to have a proper conversation. How could you start working on accurate, truthful conversation now?

Communicating Currently

The next crucial communication skill to learn is staying current with others. Rather than allowing relationships to deteriorate when something is wrong, God's Word admonishes us to go to the other person as soon as possible. Paul wrote, "Be angry and yet do not sin, do not let the sun go down on your anger" (Ephesians 4:26). Deal with things quickly! The longer you wait, the harder it is to resolve things.

Resolving problems quickly matters to the Lord. He said: "If therefore you are presenting your offering at the altar, and there remember that your brother has something against you, leave your offering there before the altar, and go your way; first be reconciled to your brother, and then come and present your offering" (Matthew 5:23-24). This is so important that you must interrupt your worship, go talk things through with the other person, and then return to worship? The Lord must think that relationships are pretty important.

Communicating to Build Up

It is also wise to learn how to speak to build up, not tear down. Ephesians 4:29 contains incredible wisdom when it comes to communication. "Let no unwholesome word proceed from your mouth, but only such a word as is good for edification according to the need of the moment, that it may give grace to those who hear." Any communication that tears others down instead of building them up is unwholesome.

A clear application of this verse is that in speaking with love to build others up, you must avoid name-calling. Calling anyone, especially those in your family, names such as "stupid," "jerk," "fat" or "lazy" hurts and causes deep damage to the relationship. Encouraging words such as "way to go," "you have talent" or "I appreciate you" are words that will build others up and will make lasting impressions on them. If you're one of those people that tend to say harsh things to others, I would urge you to practice what I tell people with a loose tongue, "Bite your tongue until it bleeds." By the way, when was the last time you purposely said something to another person to encourage him or her?

I hope you understand "let no unwholesome communication proceed from your mouth" must not be interpreted to mean we can't say hard things. The goal though, is to use words that will help others become more Christlike. Of course, at times, that means we may need to say things that will hurt at first.

Communicating Kindness and Forgiveness

Finally, speak kind, forgiving words. Lastly, Paul exhorts us to put off angry, bitter, slanderous speech and actions and instead (because of the influence of the gospel) put on kindness, tenderheartedness and forgiveness (Eph. 4:31-32). It is important to note that if we do not do as we are admonished, we are grieving the Holy Spirit (verse 30). Did you get that? God is grieved by broken relationships! This highlights again just how important relationships are to our Lord. Now would be a great time in your life to start diligently practicing communication that strengthens relationships.

Conflict Resolution Skills[55]

Liz and John not only needed to work on more godly communication, they also had poor conflict resolution skills. Closeness takes work. As I've worked with many people through the years it has become obvious to me that a lot of people know how to talk about their problems but few know how to actually bring the issues to resolution. If you don't bring the issues to resolution, bitterness just builds up and the marriage house is weakened. On the other hand, if a couple learns how to work through an issue to its conclusion, it actually strengthens the house since then they have a newfound confidence that "if we can work through *this* issue, we can work through anything."

Paul assumes that having close relationships is going to take work. He says, to be "diligent to preserve the unity of the Spirit" (4:3). The words "be diligent" imply the necessity of effort. This also implies that you will have to invest in both strong and restored relationships. If you're going to fight for something in relationships, fight for unity! Put effort into pursuing unity.

Next, move toward the other person. It is a beautiful theological truth that God through our Savior moved toward us to provide reconciliation. If accepting the gospel were left to us taking the initiative to move toward God, none of us would be saved. Scripture actually says we naturally move away from the Lord (Romans 3:11-12). Because of our sin nature we are inclined to move away from others toward self-protection. The gospel has the power to break this tendency so that we can learn to move toward reconciliation.

Many people are "escape artists" when faced with conflict. John, in our example, clammed up when faced with tensions in his relationships. Eventually, tensions built up until they blew up. John literally ran away to avoid uncomfortable situations. As you might expect, our hearts are directly linked to these "running away" attitudes and behaviors, and these usually stem from fearing what others may think if we *do* talk, or just to avoid the situation. As we deal with the false worship of our hearts, we become more motivated by love for the Lord and love for others. Therefore we desire to communicate even though we may be uncomfortable.

Just as the ultimate goal of the gospel is reconciliation, so also the ultimate goal in conflict resolution is reconciliation. Please don't let your relationships whither. To be reconciled like this, you need to be flexible as you listen to the other person's concerns and opinions. Together you can agree on a course of action that can bring total reconciliation. [56] Aren't you glad the Lord moved toward you with salvation?

Change of Heart Changed Liz and John

For Liz and John to change they needed to understand that ultimately character traits and relationship skills are impacted by the heart. Conflicts reveal our hearts. Our poor responses to tensions in relationships and our struggles with practicing healthy communication skills have an ultimate source. So, to get rid of these poor character traits you need to understand the source. "The good man out of the good treasure of his heart brings forth what is good; and the evil man out of the evil treasure brings forth what is evil; for his mouth speaks from that which is evil" (Luke 6:45).

Consider this: The next time someone does something that angers you, ask yourself some question like: "Why did this bother me so much? What was I wanting that I didn't get, and what was I getting that I didn't want?" It might reveal thoughts like, "I don't feel like talking right now." That suggests a comfort-loving heart. Or, "He isn't doing what I want him to do." That thought could reveal a controlling heart.

The following diagram has helped me think biblically about tensions in relationships and helped me think of plans to address the issues. Notice the flow of thought in this triangle starting at the bottom.[57]

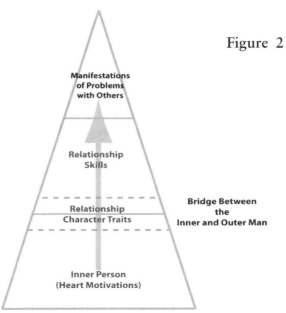

Figure 2

Manifestations of Problems with Others

Relationship Skills

Relationship Character Traits

Bridge Between the Inner and Outer Man

Inner Person (Heart Motivations)

The inner person or heart (as we saw in chapter 3) is the source from which all else flows (Proverbs 4:23). For example, ask yourself what the attitudes and actions of a controlling person are. How does he speak to others? You are probably thinking words like "harsh" or "demanding." This person probably gives commands instead of discussing issues with others. In other words, both character traits and communication skills are influenced by the controlling nature of his heart.

Using a modified diagram, let's use Liz as an example and see how her character traits and relationship skills were changed by the Lord as her heart changed. I hope you are encouraged by this. You're not stuck! Your own character traits and relationship skills can change as you too endeavor to work on change at the level of the heart.

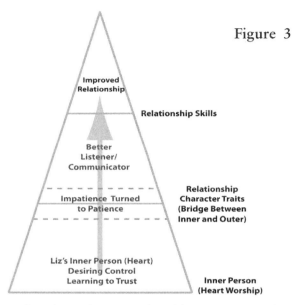

Figure 3

Improved
Relationship

Relationship Skills

Better
Listener/
Communicator

Impatience Turned
to Patience

Relationship
Character Traits
(Bridge Between
Inner and Outer)

Liz's Inner Person (Heart)
Desiring Control
Learning to Trust

Inner Person
(Heart Worship)

As Liz gave up her desire for control and began to trust the Lord with her future and with John, she became a more patient person. She stopped trying to control him, realizing that the Lord is the only One who changes hearts. This, in turn, helped her to listen to John during their conversations, resulting in a stronger relationship. As John learned not to be such a comfort lover (which had led to his running from problems) he started to move toward Liz in constructive ways, engaging her in discussions to work through issues.

As the Lord revealed things to them through his Word, they obeyed. It brought me great joy to see them respond properly, and the result was a drastic decrease in their quarrels and an increase in the closeness of their relationship.

These lists of character traits and relationship skills can be used to assess the health of all your relationships. If you are sensing a weakness in a relationship, read through the lists and do an X-ray of the relationship. Then, determine which of the items listed need improvement. I hope you will start to work on those things in the relationships you presently have. By strengthening and building wise relationships now, you are contributing to the strength of your future marriage house.

Starting to prepare now:

1. Which two of the six relationship skills do you need to work on the most?

2. Which of the character traits do you need to work on the most?

3. What could happen in your future marriage if you do not work on these things now?

4. What heart issue seems to be influencing the way you deal with conflict?

5. How does this same heart issue influence your character traits?

6. What should be the proper worship of your heart that would replace the false worship?

7. Also, consider doing the "marriage preparation project" found in Appendix 2. This project is based on the heart questions found in chapter 3 and the diagram in this chapter.

8. Write a prayer of commitment telling the Lord what you are going to work on now for the sake of your future marriage.

Questions to ask about a potential spouse:

1. How would you rate his or her communication and conflict resolution skills?

2. How does his or her family seem to communicate?

3. Which character qualities are strengths, and which are weaknesses?

4. What heart issues seem to be fueling this person's character traits and relationship skills?

Chapter 7

KNOWING WHEN YOU ARE READY FOR MARRIAGE

(What Wisdom Says)

Prepare your work outside, and make it ready for
yourself in the field; afterwards, then, build your
house.

Proverbs 24: 27

Tim and Elizabeth

I quickly became uneasy when Tim and Elizabeth arrived for premarital counseling. It seemed that they were always fighting. This
was not just getting upset with one another (which is common in all
relationships), but actually yelling. One day, in a fit of rage, Elizabeth
took off her engagement ring and threw it. Because of this event, and
how they were responding during our times together, I realized they
were not ready for the commitment of marriage. So, I tactfully told
them that in good conscience I could not be the one to marry them.
It was obvious to me there were deep issues in their lives, (individually, and in the way they had been constructing the relationship) that
would create a weak foundation for marriage. Unfortunately, they
persuaded another pastor to perform the ceremony. I really wish

that pastor had called me to find out why I would not marry them, and I have often wondered if they are still together since they clearly were not mature enough for marriage. So, how do you know when you're ready?

Cultural Wisdom

Current research "wisdom" would say that if this couple had been older when they decided to marry, they would have been more ready. In American culture both men and women are waiting for marriage until their late twenties (an average is twenty-seven for guys and twenty-six for girls). It is intriguing that secular research shows that those who wait longer have a lower divorce rate than those who marry younger. So, is just waiting longer the answer to having a stable marriage? How does age relate to actual maturity?

Others today would say that you must understand "your family of origin" to be truly ready for marriage. According to this theory, you will subconsciously carry into your marriage the rules and the understanding of roles of your family of origin. I do believe it is wise to think about how your family has influenced you, but I do not believe you are trapped into becoming like your family. You can grow and change to be more like your Savior, and as you grow, you are maturing. Isn't that the real question—is a person mature enough to get married?

Biblical Wisdom

Years ago, I found an interesting comment on marriage in Baker's Dictionary of Theology. It has some biblical insights that will us help determine when a person is ready for marriage.

> To sunder one's parental relationships and join oneself in intimate, life-long union with a person who hitherto has been a stranger demands a considerable degree of maturity—as expressed in a capacity for self-giving love, emotional stability and the capacity

to understand what is involved in committing one's life to another in marriage. Marriage is for those who have grown up. [58]

According to those criteria it's obvious that Tim and Elizabeth were definitely not ready for marriage. So, how do you know when you have grown up or are growing up? I believe the Bible would answer that when you have shown you are ready to assume the role of a biblical man or woman, you are then reaching the level of maturity necessary to be married. What defines a biblical man and woman? This is the next room to add to your future marriage house.

If we follow these criteria, there will be many ready for marriage before the mid-to-late twenties. On the other hand, some who are already married do not meet the definition of biblical manhood or womanhood, and even in their forties have not demonstrated the maturity necessary to have a stable house. Unfortunately, I've had to do marriage counseling with some of these biblically immature couples. They are neglecting key areas of their masculinity or femininity, and it shows. On the part of men, the tendency of not wanting to grow up is what some have humorously called the "Peter Pan Syndrome."

In American society, to say that battles rage over manhood and womanhood would be an understatement! The battle has been particularly fierce in defining the role of women. Some see their role as being independent, strong, invincible and determined, thinking that men have oppressed them. Most universities teach this perspective in their women's studies department. Pastor John Piper summarizes the current situation well.

> The tendency today is to stress the equality of men and women by minimizing the unique significance of our maleness and femaleness. But this depreciation of male and female personhood is a great loss. It is taking a tremendous toll on generations of young men and women who do not know what it means to be a man or woman. Confusion over the meaning of sexual personhood today is epidemic. The consequence of this confusion ... is more divorce, more homosexuality, more sexual abuse, more promiscuity, more

social awkwardness, and more emotional distress and suicide that come with the loss of God-given identity.... Little help is being given to a son's question, "Dad, what does it mean to be a man and not a woman?" Or a daughter's question, "Mom, what does it mean to be a woman and not a man?" A lot of energy is being expended today minimizing the distinctions of manhood and womanhood. But we do not hear very often what manhood and womanhood should *incline* us to do. We are adrift in a sea of confusion over sexual roles. And life is not the better for it. [59]

So, let's embark on a journey to biblically define mature manhood and womanhood. And of course, it will be "ladies first."

Characteristics of Biblical Womanhood

Who gets to define the role of women and address the views that have caused so much confusion? The answer, of course, is the Creator, and he has made himself clear in his Word. If we do not accept this, then we are left with the arbitrary views of culture and these change like the tides.

As we address the role of women, it is helpful that a main theme of Proverbs describes what a woman should and should not be. Wisdom is personified as feminine in Proverbs, and all of the characteristics of a wise woman culminate in the famous Proverbs 31 passage. This personification of Wisdom as a woman is shown in Proverbs 9, "Wisdom has built her house, she has hewn out her seven pillars; she has prepared her food, she has mixed her wine; she has also set her table."

In many places a father is teaching his son what qualities to look for in a wife, and he is also warning his son to stay away from unwise women. Proverbs 31:10 says, "An excellent wife, who can find? Her worth is far above jewels." The application to men is obvious—you should be looking for a potential wife who has the qualities extolled not only in chapter 31 but elsewhere in the book. So, men don't ignore this section, since this is the gem you are searching for.

Six Qualities Emphasized by Proverbs

1. She has a personal relationship with the Lord and is submitted to his authority and majesty.

Proverbs assumes that those who are wise "fear the Lord" (1:7). To fear God is to respect him, to be in awe of him, to desire to worship him, and to live for him. This implies a woman must know the Lord and must submit to the Lordship of Christ by admitting her need of salvation. If this person is living in awe of the Lord, then these characteristics naturally grow, just as fruit grows on a fruit tree.

Maybe you should go back and review chapter 2 to see what it means to be a follower of the Lord. Remember that the gospel is not just a message to believe, but a person to follow.

Being in awe of the Lord flows naturally into a desire to worship him and to live for his glory. In Proverbs it is assumed that the wise person believes that there is an amazing creator God who made the universe and who is thus to be worshiped with awe. This truth is crucial for women to resist the temptation to worship their husband. A practical benefit is that even when he fails, you can still be content because your hope is in the Lord and not in your husband.

2. The woman growing in godliness will be concerned about purity.

Job 28:28 puts wisdom and purity together, "Behold, the fear of the LORD, that is wisdom; and to depart from evil is understanding." The woman who is the opposite—unwise, foolish, impure (who does not depart from evil) is talked about so much in Proverbs that you can't miss it. (See chapter 5:1-6, and all of chapter 7.) However, the pure woman reserves her body for her husband and would not use her body to tempt other men.

Let's be practical and realistic about your purity and fear of the Lord. What novels do you read? What television programs and movies do you watch? What concerts do you attend? What activities do you enjoy with friends? "Fear the LORD and turn away from evil" is the pointed advice of Proverbs 3:7.

3. She knows that she lives before the Lord.

Wisdom is lived on the streets of everyday life. This is portrayed from the beginning of Proverbs when "Lady Wisdom" cries out in the busy marketplace for anyone to follow (1: 20-33). One of the reasons wise people make wise choices is because, as Proverbs 3:5-6 makes clear, in all their ways they acknowledge him. The wise woman would ask, "What does the Lord want me to do in this situation?" The remainder of Proverbs shows the wise person choosing to treat business people honestly, choosing wise friends, controlling their emotions, and staying away from situations that can pull them the wrong way. The more you develop the wise person's actions, the more you demonstrate maturity and a readiness for marriage. I hope you find in yourself this desire for wisdom. If you don't, do yourself a favor, and ask why.

4. She recognizes that the home is her special sphere of influence.

Proverbs 31 gives the description of the ultimate wise woman, "She looks well to the ways of her household, and does not eat the bread of idleness" (verse 27). She cares well for her husband, her children, and the poor of the neighborhood. The family has good food, and they have fine clothing. Her life revolves around her family so much that "her children rise up and bless her, her husband also, and he praises her saying, 'Many daughters have done nobly, but you excel them all'" (verses 28-29). Making home and family your special sphere of influence has huge rewards.

It has been devastating to the family that few young ladies, especially in the United States, have seen models of the Proverbs 31 wise woman. The standard advice given by our culture is, "You will never be fulfilled unless you have your own career." Or, "It would be wise for you to have a career because if you divorce, you will have something to support you." But, many reading this book want something better. In my years of teaching and counseling college students, I have found that many of you (contrary to cultural influences) want to be discipled by proper role models, and want to learn what it means to be "workers at home," as Paul says in Titus 2:5.

Too few young ladies enter marriage knowing the skills necessary for managing a house. To be ready for marriage, I advise you learn homemaking skills. Ideally, your mother will have taught you these skills, but if she hasn't seek guidance from a godly woman in your church.

Allow me to clarify though, this does not mean men don't help around the house. In our home everyone does chores around the house. The boys and the girls do housework, and everyone also does outside work. The girls especially focus on things that will help their mom, like preparing meals and washing the dishes. However we realize that helping with housework is good training for the boys, so that someday they can help their wives. We believe that the home is a wife's primary responsibility but the husband can also help as an act of love.

It is abundantly obvious that this wise woman helps provide for her family even though it is primarily her husbands responsibility to provide. She "considers a field and buys it; from her earnings she plants a vineyard" (verse 16). She also makes money in other ways to help provide for her family. Verse 24 tells us how, "she makes linen garments and sells belts to the tradesmen." It seems that she invests her money wisely as well. After buying a field, she makes it productive by planting a vineyard and possibly using the grapes to make wine that will produce even more money for her family. This woman has a rewarding life, and life revolves primarily around her family.

A key area for you to work on to be prepared for your future role is self-discipline. Our wise woman "looks well to the ways of her household, and does not eat the bread of idleness" (verse 27). Many women set their own schedules and therefore need to be self-motivated. The Proverbs 31 woman was motivated in her actions by her love for God and her family, which are really the two great commandments (see Matthew 22: 36-39). How could you work on self-discipline now as part of your preparation for the future? Men with godly qualities will be attracted to this.

I consider my wife to be a good example of a wise woman. She shops for the best deals possible with groceries, and she is incredible at finding wonderful clothing for us at ridiculously low prices. Along with this, when she finds things for a good price, she buys them and then lists them on eBay to make extra money for our family. Some people in our church even call her the "eBay Queen." She is disciplined as a mother, and our children know that she is tuned into their lives and loves them very much. I am a blessed man!

5. She has a balanced perspective on inward and outward beauty.

Some girls place too much emphasis on outward beauty and neglect inward beauty. On the other hand, some place hardly any emphasis on the outward appearance because they believe that their plain outward appearance is a sign of godliness. The extremes in each case should be avoided, and this is modeled by the wise woman of chapter 31. "Charm is deceitful and beauty is vain, but a woman who fears the LORD, she shall be praised" (verse 30). This verse, taken alone, could imply that she neglected her appearance. But verse 22 informs us, "She makes coverings for herself; her clothing is fine linen and purple." She dressed beautifully, but she balanced her outward appearance with her inward beauty.

Men are strongly warned not to be seduced by a woman that just emphasizes outward beauty. "As a ring of gold in a swine's snout, so is a beautiful woman who lacks discretion" (Proverbs 11:22). I can't help but remember the experience of one of our sons. He went to a fair where he saw the "world's largest pig." It weighed over 1,000 pounds and had a snout a foot long! Can you imagine the ugliness of that animal? No number of gold rings in its nose would enhance its beauty. That's the point. It's pointless for a woman to be beautiful, if she doesn't have the characteristics of wisdom. The pig ruins the beauty of the ring, as the lack of character ruins the beauty of a woman.

Ladies, how do you want to attract men—with your body or your character and Christlike personality? Maybe you need to understand that men *will* be attracted to the form of your body. Even godly men struggle with keeping their thoughts pure if a girl dresses in tight or otherwise inappropriate clothing. Please do not have the attitude of, "That's their problem. I should be able to dress how I want and they should just keep their eyes to themselves." I agree with you that men need to discipline their eyes, but you also have an obligation to dress in a way that shows love to your Christian brothers so that they do not stumble because of you. Your primary goal should be to attract them to your inward beauty, but, as I heard someone wisely say, "If the barn needs painting, paint it!"

6. She is a faithful blessing to her husband.

A young lady who is preparing for marriage will recognize that she is called of God to complement her husband, as Eve did Adam (Genesis 2:18). A wife's first family responsibility is to her husband. "An excellent wife, who can find? For her worth is far above jewels. The heart of her husband trusts in her, and he will have no lack of gain. She does him good and not evil all the days of her life" (Proverbs 31:10-23). The word "excellent" brings many ideas to mind. The same word describes David's "mighty men of valor," and Ruth's reputation: "All my people in the city know that you are a woman of excellence" (Ruth 3:11). Notice what the verse *doesn't* say, "An excellent mother who can find?" Motherhood seems to come naturally to many women, but being an excellent wife is something that many have to learn.

When you reach the place where you, and others, are seeing these wise, biblical qualities and principles unfolding in your life, you are more ready for marriage. The degree to which they are evident in your life is the degree to which you are ready to successfully assume the responsibilities of marriage. On the other hand, a woman who marries without an understanding of biblical womanhood lacks the maturity to handle her new responsibilities well; however, the more she has these principles incorporated into her life, the more she will contribute to the success of her marriage. This principle does not mean that a woman must be perfect before beginning marriage, because one can always grow in wisdom. As I said before, there are always home improvement projects. Please don't get hung up on the *quantity* of these characteristics. Just start working on them!

Maybe you're saying at this point, "This seems unfair, what about the men?" Men, it is time to turn our attention to you. I've heard many young women lament, "Where are the godly guys?" To answer that question, we have to find the true description of a godly man.

Characteristics of a Biblical Man

How do you become a man? Is there a special ceremony that must take place? Does it occur when you reach a certain age? American culture says you're an adult when you turn eighteen, but does that make you a man? During the marriage ceremony, does something mystically happen and transform you into a man!

One year on Father's Day, I received a card from my children that read something like, "Show everyone how much of a man you are by wearing these cool tattoos." When I opened it, the card included four rub-on tattoos. My favorite one had a heart in the middle with tools surrounding it, and it said, "Real men love hardware stores." That's the one I chose to wear. Does this help us understand manhood: a real man is tough and has tattoos? You know, like those Harley types. How would you define manhood?

Biblically defining manhood is not easy because we don't have one book, like Proverbs, that provides us with a composite. This task is also more difficult because the word "man" is used over two thousand times in the Bible, sometimes as a generic term for all mankind, and sometimes referring to males in particular. To define manhood we need to put together a composite from Scripture—that sounds quite daunting. It helps though, that we have the example of the perfect man in our Lord. Ladies, as we begin, let me remind you not to ignore this, since this is the kind of man you are to be looking for.

On my office wall I have three pictures that remind me what it means to be a pastor, and also what it means to be a man. The pictures all show a shepherd fulfilling his responsibility to his flock. In one picture he is leading them, and they are following. In another he is fighting off a hungry pack of ferocious wolves. In the third he is acting as a comforter to one of his sheep. Keep these pictures in mind as we try to understand biblical manhood.

So how do we define manhood? One definition I appreciate is, "A godly man has a sense of responsibility to lead, provide for and protect women and family." [60] I used this with my sons to help them understand what they were to aim for as men. Each of them is aiming to be a shepherd in his home.

A Godly Man Has a Sense of Responsibility to Be a Leader

Throughout Scripture, God calls men to lead wisely, which is leading lovingly. In the book of Ephesians, men and women are told, "For the husband is the head of the wife, as Christ also is the head of the church, He Himself being the Savior of the body" (Ephesians 5:23). Christ leads the church as the Chief Shepherd, and men follow his example as those who shepherd their families in ways that reflect Christlikeness. If you have not had a good example of what this means, don't be discouraged. The Lord has left you sufficient information in his Word and has given his Holy Spirit to teach you how to be a godly leader. In addition, you could find an older, godly man who would be willing to mentor you. Let's think in more detail what it means to be a leader.

First, a leader is a servant. [61] Our Savior was a servant, which sets him apart from other leaders. In John 13 he demonstrated leadership by washing his disciples' feet. As a servant, he was setting an example for all to follow, especially men. Mark 10:45 says, "For even the Son of Man did not come to be served, but to serve, and to give His life a ransom for many." Earlier he had said to his disciples, "Whoever wishes to become great among you shall be your servant" (Mark 10:43). As men, you are called to demonstrate this kind of leadership. Sacrificial leadership is demonstrated by being the greatest servant, not by being the greatest ruler. Although many men think that being a leader means exerting pressure like a boss, this behavior does not coincide with the teaching that a godly man is a servant. Being a loving servant enhances your leadership, so that when you give directions, your wife and children will know that it comes from a heart of love and service. One way of assessing your readiness for marriage is when you sense that you have the desire to serve others. Are you ready to lovingly lead a family?

Second, a leader has the responsibility to take the initiative. A sign of growing maturity is the willingness to assume responsibility— when he sees something that needs to be done, he does it. This also is following the example of Christ. He saw our greatest need and he took the initiative, at his own personal sacrifice, to come into the world and to die for our sin. This means that a leader will be active, not passive. As a Christian man, you must show responsibility by taking the initiative in areas that would demonstrate biblical priorities. Biblical priorities include things like leading others in worship, discipling others, and faithfully attending worship with your church family.

Someday you will be responsible for all these family activities. You can tell that a young man is maturing when he starts to take the initiative in areas like these instead of remaining passive.

The idea that servant leadership is shown in taking the initiative is stated well in the following quotation:

> The leadership pattern would be less than Biblical if the wife in general was having to take the initiative in prayer at mealtime, and get the family out of bed for worship on Sunday morning, and gather the family for devotions, and discuss what moral standards will be required of the children, and confer about financial priorities.... A wife may initiate the discussion and planning of any one of these, but if she becomes the one who senses the general responsibility for this pattern of initiative while her husband is passive, something contrary to Biblical masculinity and femininity is in the offing. [62]

What could you work on now to start getting ready to be an active servant leader in your own family? Is your reputation one of diligence or "taking it easy?" And, when was the last time you purposely did something to serve someone?

A Godly Man Has a Sense of Responsibility to Provide for a Wife and Family

Guys, you can tell a man is more ready for marriage when he gets more serious about a good work ethic. Genesis 2 and 3 make it abundantly clear that Adam was designed to be the "keeper of the garden." 1 Timothy 5:8 reinforces that: "But if any man does not provide for his own, and especially for those of his household, he has denied the faith, and he is worse than an unbeliever."

Here again, Jesus serves as a model for men as providers. In the Gospels, he is the "bread of life" and the "living water." He makes sure that his followers are provided for abundantly. Paul, following the example of Christ, was also a hard worker, and he cared for the spiritual needs of those for whom he ministered (1 Thessalonians 2:9). You must learn how to work hard, and you must learn how to make a living to provide for a family before you become involved romantically. This principle is implied in Proverbs 24:27, "Prepare your work outside, and make it ready for yourself in the field; afterwards, then, build your house."

It would be ideal for you to know what your gifts and talents are, and what career you are going to pursue before you get married. You can be deeply in love with your wife but romance won't pay the bills. As part of your preparation for adulthood I would urge you to consider what the Lord has designed you to do. It seems that many men have no sense of calling or mission in life. Because of this they job hop, which then leads to instability in a family.

The more you develop a strong work ethic the closer you are to being ready for marriage. What could you do to start working on this now? Your parents might faint, but how about, on your own initiative, you do some work that you see needs to be done around your home.

A Godly Man Has a Responsibility to Protect

We men all seem to have a little bit of Rambo in us. It is instinctive in most men to want to protect women and children. For example, it would be unseemly for a man to hide when his wife or children were in danger. Our Savior is the model for men. He fought the ultimate enemy (sin) and its chief representative (Satan). He was the ultimate warrior, and he won! Men are called to "love your wives, just as Christ also loved the church and gave Himself up for her (Ephesians 5:25)." Protection is a key responsibility for men.

Consider that your future home is your castle and you are the guard. You are called to protect your castle. There are a lot of home invaders other than burglars. Consider these questions: what will you allow through the gate of television? What will you allow through the gate of music? As a future father, how will you protect your daughters from the wrong kind of men? How will you train your boys to be knights alongside of you?

Some men desire to be married, but they don't want the responsibility of leading, providing for and protecting, so they choose living with someone who will provide the benefits of marriage without its responsibilities. God's Word condemns this lifestyle. Men who want romance without the responsibilities of marriage are not ready for this commitment. They are also settling for a lesser form of intimacy.

Deeper intimacy comes when a woman knows she has married a man who is a loving leader, loving provider and loving protector. This is the kind of man she can feel safe with and trust. The intimacy that can occur in this type of relationship is worth all of the work.

As we have seen throughout this chapter, readiness is not connected so much to age as it is to your maturity. When you are reaching the maturity that encompasses the characteristics of womanhood and manhood, you will be ready for marriage. Much of that depends on you. Whether you are a man or a woman, there are plenty of characteristics that you can be building into your life now as you continue to add rooms to your future marriage house.

And, by the way, I do love hardware stores!

Starting to prepare now:

1. Of the characteristics given for biblical womanhood or manhood, which two are your strongest? Which two are your weakest? What can you do to work on the weak characteristics?

2. What questions do you have about biblical manhood or womanhood?

3. What is hindering you from accepting your design as a man or woman?

4. Write a prayer of commitment telling the LORD that you are willing to work on the characteristics of mature manhood or womanhood.

Questions to ask about a potential spouse:

1. What is his or her understanding of family roles?

2. To what degree do you see evidence of maturing womanhood or manhood in this person's life?

Women: Could you trust this man's leadership?

Men: Do you believe this woman would follow your leadership?

Chapter 8

WISDOM AND GOD'S WILL

(How Will You Know the Right Person?)

The LORD is my shepherd.... He leads me in paths of righteousness for His name's sake.

Psalm 23:1, 3

My wife Rose had a difficult experience when she was in college; one boy was absolutely convinced that the Lord had told him that he would marry her. There was a little problem though. The Lord had not given her the same message, and she was not interested. He was also certain that Rose was sending him messages through her roommate. If the roommate smiled at him, he knew that everything was all right in his relationship with Rose. After finding this out, both the roommate and Rose made sure they did not smile when he was around. I happened to be his roommate at the time (before Rose and I had developed a relationship), and I realized that he was so worried about a girl that his sleep was disturbed and his schoolwork was affected. I had no idea who the girl was who had affected him to the point of distraction.

The next year, Rose and I began to develop a relationship, and soon we believed the Lord was leading us to marry. When we announced our engagement, after having dated for about nine months, the news caused panic in the young man. Later he told me how God had told him to marry Rose. I asked him what he was going to do because she was not interested in him. He could not comprehend that possibility; he was convinced that he had received a message from the Lord. I asked him whether he was going to drag her down the aisle, and he answered, "If I have to." He was so persistent in trying to contact Rose even after we graduated that we had to warn the ushers not to admit him to the wedding if he showed up. At the time, I was angry and even somewhat afraid of what he might do. Now, the whole experience strikes me as kind of funny. I get a picture in my mind of a Viking capturing and carrying off his bride. Praise God that painful chapter in our lives is closed, and we have not heard from him since.

How Does God Lead?

Incidents like this create questions about knowing God's will regarding the one you should marry. Does God speak to you audibly, or will he let you know through some sign? Will you have some inner feeling that this is the right one? I am asked about this over and over when I talk to single college students about their fears or concerns regarding marriage. For example, they might ask, "How can I find the right one?" "What if I miss the right one?" "Is there only one soul mate?" Or, "What if I wake up one day and realize I married a weirdo?" For the most part, the questions boil down to, "How do I find the right one?" And, "Could I marry the wrong one?"

As we have been building this marriage house, we have been seeing the importance of building it with wisdom based on Scripture. I hope you have understood that when uncertainty arises about whom you should marry, you can go to God's Word for direction. As Psalm 119:105 says, "Your word is a lamp to my feet and a light to my path." This verse implies uncertainty. The path is dark and unclear, and it seems frightening. Maybe you are feeling this way about the uncertainties of marriage and whom to marry in particular, but the Lord, through his Word, desires to reassure you.

I believe that you can be encouraged though, because God has promised to give you principles to direct you like a lamp for your feet. Your job is to continue to learn those principles, and trust him. To be convinced that he is trustworthy, you must understand his character and how he works in his universe. You need to see that he is firmly in control of all things, so you can rest instead of worry.

God Is Sovereign

For our souls to stay calm when we are making major decisions, we need to realize that there is a God who is far bigger than we are, who cares for us, is involved in all the affairs of our lives, and who keeps his promises. Scripture clearly says, "God is not a man, that He should lie, nor a son of man, that He should repent; has He said and will He not do it? Or has He spoken, and will He not make it good?" (Numbers 23:19).

He Is in Control of all Nature

How big is God? He is so big that he is in control of all nature. As an example of this Isaiah quotes the Lord: "'To whom then will you liken Me that I should be his equal?' says the Holy One. 'Lift up your eyes on high and see who has created these stars, the One who leads forth their host by number, He calls them all by name'" (Isaiah 40: 25-26). Think of it—he is so great that he names each star in the sky! These verses teach that he is like a mighty general who could lead forth the host of the stars as an army if he desired to do so. They would all report for duty! [63]

His control of nature is so complete that Colossians says that, "He is before all things, and in Him all things hold together" (Colossians 1:17). Does he care about your future marriage? I believe the answer to that will become clearer as we learn about his sovereignty.

He Is in Control of all Nations

God is not only sovereign over nature, he is also the ruler of the nations. He has a plan that is being worked out for all of history. History is truly "his story." Daniel extols the virtues of our God when he says, "Let the name of God be blessed forever and ever, for wisdom and power belong to Him. And it is He who changes the times and the epochs; he removes kings and establishes kings; He gives wisdom to wise men, and knowledge to men of understanding.

It is e who reveals the profound and hidden things" (Daniel 2:20-22). You may still be asking, "Does he care about me as a person and care about my marriage?"

The clear message of Scripture is that the answer is, Yes! He cares about individuals. David wrote in Psalm 139: 1-3, "O Lord, You have searched me and known me. You know when I sit down and when I rise up; You understand my thought from afar. You scrutinize my path and my lying down, and are intimately acquainted with all my ways." Luke records the Lord as saying, "Indeed the very hairs of your head are all numbered. Do not fear ..." (Luke 12:7).

Your soul can rest in him, because he is all powerful, he does care and can give you the wisdom to choose the right spouse. Just as with everything else, he plans, and that relationship will occur in the right timing.

He Is Your Shepherd

There is more good news about how he cares for you. This sovereign God is not only in control of all things, but he also promises to be *your* shepherd. If you have become a follower of Jesus Christ, then you are part of his flock, and he cares very much for his sheep. The Lord himself said in John 10, "I am the good shepherd; the good shepherd lays down His life for the sheep" (verse 11). "I am the good shepherd; and I know My own, and My own know Me" (verse 14). These verses make it very plain that he cares so much for his flock that he was willing to die.

The Old Testament includes many promises about the Lord being a shepherd to his people. Here are four examples: "But He led forth His own people like sheep, and guided them in the wilderness like a flock; and He led them safely, so that they did not fear; but the sea engulfed their enemies" (Psalm 78:52-53). "Oh give ear, Shepherd of Israel, Thou who dost lead Joseph like a flock" (Psalm 80:1). "Save Thy people, and bless Thine inheritance; be their shepherd also, and carry them forever" (Psalm 28:9). "Like a shepherd He will tend His flock, in His arm He will gather the lambs, and carry them in His bosom; He will gently lead the nursing ewes" (Isaiah 40:11). Think through the implications of these promises. I hope they begin to reassure you.

He Knows You, Cares for You and Does What Is Best

In Psalm 80:1 we are told that Jesus leads Joseph like a flock. He uses a personal name to state his relationship with his people. Joseph is representing the whole nation of Israel here, but it also shows that God knows people by their first names. He knows you in that way also.

Remember, he knows every time you sit down and rise up. These verses assure us that he cares for and leads his flock and even carries his sheep. Isn't it comforting to think that he knows you by name and that he is involved in the specifics of each individual life? Here's the hard part. Will you choose to believe it?

Leads gently

As a shepherd, he leads his flock in a loving way. He is so gentle that he is pictured as carrying little lambs and gently leading their nursing mothers (Isaiah 40:11). He never leads his flock to a dangerous place. Even though things enter our lives that would make it seem that he does not love us, nothing would ever violate his wise and loving character.

Leads those who trust

Scripture also makes it clear that he leads those who trust him. Trusting the Lord shows our relationship with the Lord and our dependence upon him. It is well known that trust is a vital part of any healthy relationship. "And without faith it is impossible to please Him, for he who comes to God must believe that He is and that He is a rewarder of those who seek Him" (Hebrews 11:6). Realize that you were created to be in a dependent relationship, and therefore your trust in him is fulfilling your natural design. In particular, your prayer life shows how dependent you are; if you are not talking with him, you must not think you need him.

Leads through Scripture

Lastly, and maybe most importantly because of the subject of this chapter, he leads us primarily through wisdom gained by knowing and applying Scripture. "All Scripture is inspired by God and profitable for teaching, for reproof, for correction, for training in righteousness; that the man of God may be adequate, equipped for every good work" (2 Timothy 3: 16-17). Notice that these verses do not say that God's Word equips you for most or some good works; Scripture equips you for every good work. This includes choosing a spouse wisely. I want to make it very clear, wisdom is gained by knowing and applying Scripture, rather than being led by subjective experiences.

Instead, as a Christ-follower, you are on an amazing journey as your Sovereign is orchestrating the events of your life, and you are applying the principles of Scripture. He is working out his purposes even when you do not feel like he is there. You do not live a haphazard life since he promises to direct your path (Proverbs 3:5-6).

His Part, Our Part

It is clear from Scripture that this amazing God does have a specific plan for your life and this would include a specific spouse. If you choose to trust God it can result in freedom from worry. You focus on your responsibilities, and God focuses on his. If you spend time focusing on God's areas of responsibility, you are wasting your time, because there is nothing you can do to change his will or speed up the process. He is going to lead you to your future spouse.

A pattern emerges here. His job is to be the shepherd, and our job is to follow, by living according to his Word, growing in wisdom and trusting him. Often problems come because we do not trust. We worry, are full of fear and come up with our own plans; then our plans get us in trouble. Our attitude should be like David's. In Psalm 28:7 he says, "The LORD is my strength and my shield; my heart trusts in Him, and I am helped; therefore my heart exults, and with my song I shall thank Him."

We Must Choose to Believe

As I've already mentioned, we must choose to believe, but let's unpack that a little more. One of my favorite authors defines *trust* this way. "Trust is not a passive state of mind. It is a vigorous act of the soul by which we choose to lay hold on the promises of God and cling to them despite the adversity that at times seeks to overwhelm us." [64] Many things could be explored within this definition, but I'll emphasize just one. Trust is a struggle with your own soul to believe God's Word. Your inner person wants you to believe lots of false things, but Scripture is the trustworthy guide.

So, let me ask you, are you relying on his strength to help you wait for a spouse? Do you believe he is your shield to protect you from bad choices? Do you trust him that he knows best, or are you insisting on making your own plans?

I really appreciate what a college student once wrote to me. I'm including it here because I suspect that many can relate to her concern.

> Dear Pastor,
>
> Another thing I would like to talk about is holiness; holiness in thoughts, holiness in actions, holiness in speech, and holiness in desires. Holiness in desires leads me to something I would like to talk about again. I am realizing more and more … that my job right now is to WAIT [her emphasis] for the right guy to come along, but the problem is that my heart does not really want to do that. In fact, it really DOES NOT [her emphasis] want to do that. Fortunately (Providentially), there isn't anybody that I think is the right kind of person around right now, so that makes it easier. So, if we could talk about waiting, and waiting patiently, and what to do in the meantime, that would be great.

You Are Not Going to Hear a Voice

Some think that they will hear voices, have dreams or encounter some other mysterious manifestation that will lead them to a future spouse. Those who base their decisions on these subjective occurrences rather than on Scripture place themselves under tremendous pressure. Having a mystical view of God's guidance leads to worry about whether they are in or out of God's will. They are constantly concerned about interpreting the circumstances of life to determine if God is speaking to them or showing them something. Instead of enjoying their relationship with the Lord and growing in wisdom, they live in bondage to their feelings and circumstances. I would urge you to consider that such feelings and impressions are not reliable.

I know that some people live this way because this is how I used to be. I remember being in great anguish trying to figure out which college the Lord wanted me to attend. I was always looking for a sign or a feeling to indicate that I was making the right decision. Instead of enjoying my relationship with the Lord, I thought he was playing a nerve-wracking game of hide and seek.

The idea that feelings and impressions are not reliable is something that has been noted by many throughout church history. Jonathan Edwards was the greatest revival preacher of the Great Awakening (1730s-1740s), and many also consider him to be America's greatest theologian. During the Great Awakening, many strange things happened in the revival meetings. Loud outbursts, fainting and wailing were common as emotions ran high and as God convicted individuals of their sin. Edwards received a lot of criticism from his fellow ministers for allowing these strange experiences and emotions to continue in the meetings. This criticism drove him to study Scripture to learn to discern if the Holy Spirit was speaking to someone or if they were being deceived by their emotions or possibly their heart. Based upon this study of Scripture he wrote the following:

> We are not to expect that the Spirit of God should guide us infallibly as He did the apostles. Yet otherwise godly people fail to understand this. Many godly persons have undoubtedly in this and other ages exposed themselves to woeful delusions, by a tendency to lay too much weight on subjective impulses and impressions, as if they were immediate revelations from God to signify something future, or to direct them where to go and what to do. [65]

Scripture warns us to be careful of placing experiences and voices above the written Word of God. In 2 Peter we are told about an extraordinary event: Peter wrote,

> For we did not follow cleverly devised tales when we made known to you the power and coming of our Lord Jesus Christ, but we

were eyewitnesses of His majesty. For when He received honor and glory from God the Father, such an utterance as this was made to Him by the Majestic Glory, "This is my beloved Son with whom I am well-pleased"—and we ourselves heard this utterance made from heaven when we were with Him on the holy mountain. (2 Peter 1:16-18)

Peter is relating how he, James, and John had the awesome experience of seeing the Lord Jesus transformed right before their eyes. The Lord's glory was revealed to them, and they heard God speak from heaven. Peter says that this event is proof that he was not following a myth (see Matthew 17:1-13 for the whole story).

What Peter writes next is absolutely amazing, and should capture the attention of those who live by inner impressions and by hearing voices for God's guidance. "And so we have the prophetic word made more sure, to which you do well to pay attention as to a lamp shining in a dark place, until the day dawns and the morning star arises in your hearts." He is saying that we would be wise to pay closer attention to the revealed Word of God ("The prophetic word made more sure") than to personal experience—even a personal experience like seeing Jesus revealed in all his glory! Peter is confident that Scripture is more reliable because it was given to writers who were moved by the Holy Spirit. Why would he write this? Peter was warning the church against false teachers who were claiming to have new messages from God.

There is also another practical reason why we all need to be warned about living by impressions. Our feelings and impressions are unstable. God's Word is absolutely reliable. God has written it down; he has gone on record with his promises. Since it is recorded, it is trustworthy.

The story of the rich man and Lazarus found in Luke 16 is another example of the superiority of the Word of God compared to experiences. The rich man dies and then begs Abraham to send Lazarus back from the grave to tell his brothers to repent before it is too late. Listen to Abraham's astounding answer. "But he said to him, 'If they do not listen to Moses and the Prophets, neither will they be persuaded if someone rises from the dead'" (verse 31). In other words, they may have the incredible experience of being talked to by someone who has risen from the dead, but listening to the Word of God (Moses and the Prophets) is more important and should be enough. They do not need the experience; they have Scripture.

How do we then properly interpret the experiences of life? As I mentioned earlier, many people believe that God leads by direct (audible) communication or by "opening and closing doors of opportunity."

Your experiences and circumstances have a proper place

Since we have honored God's Word by showing that the Lord guides us primarily through his Word, we can now consider the place of God's intervention in our lives through circumstances. Historically, this is called the doctrine of "providence."

When we think of something providential, we think of something occurring for our good. When Rose and I were in graduate school, we had our first child. We lived on a limited budget, and our child became sick. We had only twenty dollars for groceries, but we also had to have medical care for our baby, so without telling anyone about our situation, we took our daughter to the doctor. When we returned home, we found two bags of groceries and an envelope containing twenty dollars. God had providentially intervened in our circumstances.

To have a well-rounded view of God's providential intervention in our lives, we must consider some cautions. Providence may also mean that God intervenes by allowing temporary pain to occur because it is for our own good. Romans 8:28 says, "And we know that God causes all things to work together for our good to those who love God, to those who are called according to His purposes." God's sovereign purposes are working in your life (even in broken relationships) because he is more interested in your holiness than in your happiness. He knows that you will be happy in the end if you deal with your unholy actions that keep you from being like his Son (Romans 8:28). Holiness leads to true happiness.

You must not, however, be mystical about circumstances. It would be easy to have a "the gods are not happy" attitude. When something negative happens in your life, it does not mean that God is angry with you. All circumstances, feelings, impressions, open doors and closed doors must be interpreted in light of wisdom given through God's Word. Without this view, you will make unwise decisions and forget the wise principles for evaluating a potential spouse.

In other words, God's Word is divine revelation; circumstances are not. If you do not have this high view of Scripture, you will find yourself making bad decisions; you will tend to pursue opportunities just because they appeared instead of evaluating them.

For example, maybe you spent time pouring your heart out to the Lord asking him to provide a relationship with someone, and that very day you walk out of class and see someone sitting in front of you reading his or her Bible. It would be very easy for someone desperate for a relationship to interpret this as a sign from God, and ignore all the principles for evaluating a potential spouse. On the other hand, for the person pursuing wisdom and a satisfied relationship with the Lord, this may be a person the Lord wants him to meet. He can talk to her and begin to evaluate whether it would be a wise relationship. God lovingly encourages you to be wise in your choice, and he has given you a manual (his Word) so that you can grow in wisdom. He knows whom you will marry, and he has this factored into his plan for your life. James Petty summarizes this well:

> The Bible teaches that (1) God does have one specific plan for your life and (2) the events and choices of your life irresistibly and sovereignly work that plan in every detail…. It has all your mistakes, blindnesses, and sins accounted for in advance. These truths are included in what is known as the doctrine of providence. Without understanding providence, we will never be able to think clearly about God's daily involvement with our lives. Much of the confusion about God's guidance in Christian circles is caused by a lack of understanding of this historic doctrine. [66]

Isn't this reassuring? God does his part by being the Sovereign God of the universe who is involved in your life and cares for you as part of his flock. He also leads through circumstances and his will is being accomplished as he leads you through life's circumstances. You do your part by seeking wisdom and choosing to believe his promises and trusting him, which results in resting in him and growing in wisdom instead of worrying.

Answering Common Questions

Is there only one right person for you to marry?

The answer is no and yes. How do you like that for a contradictory message! From our human perspective the answer is no. I believe that this is an area of Christian liberty. God does not give a specific directive about the one person for you, except that the person must be a believer and that you must choose with biblical wisdom. Gary Friesen succinctly makes this point; "Apart from that single imperative, Scripture gives no other commands directly related to the selection of a marriage partner. As in all other decisions, however, the Christian is required to make the wisest possible choice. Accordingly, the first 'woman' a Christian man should court is Wisdom!" (Proverbs 2:1-6). [67]

But, from God's perspective, the answer is yes. God's sovereign plan already includes whom you will marry, and even though it is mysterious, his plan is going to happen. You are not called to try desperately to figure it out. You are called to trust him and rest in him and use wisdom.

What about the idea of finding my "soul mate?"

The term "soul mate" has become a popular term to describe what people want in a spouse. They are looking for a kindred spirit, one who is their best friend, the one person who fits them best. Or, as "The State of Our Unions" report said, "A spiritualized union of souls." [68] I believe this is a naïve, fantasy-world idea. I believe you can have a soul mate, but this closeness will not be evident at the beginning of your relationship. Believing that there is only one right soul mate can lead to a frustrating quest of finding the person who ideally fits you instead of becoming the person God wants you to be. Becoming soul mates can happen only as you both practice the principles from

God's Word. My wife and I are soul mates resulting from years of commitment, using proper relationship skills and understanding roles. Don't go on a quest to find your soul mate. Go on a quest to find wisdom!

What about getting to know someone through online dating or matching services? [69]

Many methodologies to find a spouse are being used around the world. The question then becomes one of whether or not the methodology violates any biblical principles. The two concerns I have with online matching services are 1) the emphasis on finding someone who *meets your needs* and 2) the potential for not getting to know the real person. I don't believe you will ever find any one person who could be the perfect need-meeter for your life. (Chapter 3 discussed this in more detail.) Wisdom also tells me that if I don't see this person in the context of other relationships I will get a distorted view of the person. You must spend time with the person as he or she interacts with others, or else you cannot be sure who the true person is. For example, how does this person deal with life? Can you tell that through electronic communication in an online conversation? But if these services are used with wisdom they may be a great tool. The next chapter looks more closely at various methodologies.

What about "putting out a fleece" (as Gideon did) to confirm God's will?

Judges 6 records that God called Gideon to defeat the Midianites and promised to be with him. Gideon was insecure, and he put a fleece of wool outside on the ground two times to get confirmation from God. The Lord was patient with Gideon, although he had already given him a clear directive.

I believe the use of a fleece is not a standard for Christians to follow, though many try to do that. The Bible records that incident to show God's graciousness in spite of Gideon's insecure faith.

God may be patient with you and confirm his will through some direct evidence, but he desires that you take him at his word and live by faith, applying the principles of Scripture. When God commands you to do something in Scripture, you do not need a "fleece" to confirm it

Will God lead me to my spouse as he did with Isaac and Rebekah?

The reason the passage with Isaac and Rebekah is given is to show that God was keeping his promise to Abraham that he would be the father of many nations. Isaac had to have a special bride because the line of the Messiah was being developed. This passage was not meant to set a precedent for how to go about finding a spouse or how God will dramatically lead you. The situation was unique, showing that God is faithful and will go to great lengths to fulfill his special promises to his covenant people (see Numbers 23:19).

If God is leading my life, why aren't things going better?

If you have been hurt because of bad relationships, or if you are lonely and tired of waiting to marry, meditate on passages of Scripture such as 1 Corinthians 10:13 and Psalm 27. God promises not to give you more than you can endure, and he will provide a way to help you persevere. God is always good, and he always has good purposes for what he allows you to go through. His timing is perfect. You can trust him.

Starting to prepare now:

1. How is the view of knowing God's will, that was explained in this chapter, different from what you have been taught?

2. Which view do you believe is the most biblical, and why?

3. Write a prayer of praise to the Lord for being your shepherd, and include a commitment that you will follow the wise principles of Scripture for discerning God's will instead of following feelings and impressions.

4. What questions do you have that were not answered by this chapter?

Questions to ask about a potential spouse:

1. Does this person seek the Lord through biblical wisdom or through mystical signs?

2. Does he or she trust the Lord as his or her shepherd?

Chapter 9

WISDOM AND METHODOLOGIES

(Choosing the Right Tool for Building)

Whatever I command you, you shall be careful to do;
you shall not add to nor take away from it.

Deuteronomy 12:32

When you're doing construction projects it's always wise to choose the right tool for the job. In fact, contractors are known for their accumulation of tools; they look for excuses to buy new ones. It's not unusual for a builder to own a garage or storage yard full of tools. If you don't have the correct tool or you have a poorly made tool, it can cause major frustration. Here's a story that illustrates how you can create a lot of extra work by not having the correct tool.

One of the many construction projects I helped with was a two-story garage. Part of the project was to install pipes underground connecting the house with the garage. We were building this garage during the middle of summer on the East Coast, so it was hot and humid. I mean really, really hot! I was a teenager, and all I remember is that my father told me we were going to a use pick and shovel to dig a ditch between the garage and house through hard-packed dirt. It was so hot that we could dig only a few inches and then stop for a drink of water. This was some of the hardest work I ever remember doing in my life. I would dig a little while my father rested and then he would dig while I rested. This was not a shallow ditch either, it had to be deep enough so that the pipe in the bottom would not freeze during the winter. Much to my relief, we finally got it done.

As I reflect back on this incident, I ask myself this question: Why didn't my father use a backhoe? A backhoe would have been the perfect machine, specifically designed to dig ditches. I'm sure my father had a legitimate reason (which he never told me), but it sure would've saved a lot of time and effort if we had used the right tool.

Options of Tools

In a world where many methodologies are promoted for finding a spouse, it's crucial that you use the correct tool, and that it is well made. I want to help you build your future marriage house as wisely as possible, so let's evaluate the options. Here is a list of the methods being touted as the way to find the right spouse. Because you can find complete books on each of these methodologies, I don't need to explain each in detail. My main goal here is to evaluate each one biblically and give clear principles for adding another person to your life.

- Cohabitation
- Psychological wisdom
- Traditional Dating
- Betrothal
- Courtship
- Matching services

Each method has its proponents claiming their way is best, and some even claim their way is God's way.

Evaluating the Options

A building code usually sets the standard for a construction project. As we have seen throughout this book, the building code for your marriage house is God's Word. Without this standard it would be easy to use whatever methodology the culture promotes without discernment. Some of these methodologies clearly violate biblical principles, while others are, to varying degrees, wise or unwise. But, generally speaking, Scripture does not promote one method over another. Scriptural principles apply in whatever situations (or culture) you find yourself.

You probably agree that we should use the Bible as our standard, but the next obvious question is how to do that without getting too complicated. Whole books could be written on evaluating each of these methodologies. I believe Deuteronomy 12:32 can help us here. It provides us with an "evaluation principle" and helps us see how serious it is to take away from God's Word or add to God's Word. "Whatever I command you, you shall be careful to do; you shall not add to nor take away from it." Moses is commanding the people of God to take God's Word seriously and not to tamper with it. It is a serious thing to ignore Scripture, and equally serious to go beyond God's requirements and add to the Bible things God never intended. (See also Deuteronomy 4:2 and Revelation 22:18-19.) Our Lord confronted the religious leaders of his day on this issue. He said, "But in vain do they worship Me, teaching as their doctrines the precepts of men" (Matthew 15:9). The extra-biblical, legalistic standards the religious leaders added to Scripture were like heavy weights upon the people. Let's see how each of these methodologies potentially adds to or takes away from Scripture.

Cohabitation

First I will begin with cohabitation since over 50 percent of singles in the United States use a combination of cohabitation and traditional dating to find a husband or wife. This is the predominant pathway to marriage both in the United States and many countries around the world. The typical scenario would be something like this: You meet each other, are attracted to one another, and then after being with each other for a while, which would involve going out on dates and being involved sexually, you decide to live together. Many times cohabitation is done to save money, and also to "test drive" the relationship to see if he or she is the person you would like to *eventually* marry.

Adding to and taking away

I believe this method both adds to *and* takes away from Scripture. Most significantly, singles who live together take away from Scripture (and each other) by not practicing sexual purity, a direct violation of 1 Thessalonians 4:1-8. But also consider that when Scripture encourages a man to leave his father and mother and cleave to someone, it is always to a wife. As we saw earlier, this principle of leaving and cleaving (Genesis 2:24) was for the purpose of setting up a new household. Accordingly, a couple first gets married, and then they set up the household, not the other way around.

This tool, cohabitation, is a poorly made tool because it also takes away from Scripture by directly attacking the stability of marriage—it encourages a lack of commitment. One of the most basic biblical ingredients of marriage is, "I promise to be committed to you no matter what." This level of commitment is modeled in Scripture by Christ's covenant love for his bride the church, which we are told to emulate.

Consider the findings of a study titled, "Why Men Won't Commit: Exploring Young Men's Attitudes about Sex, Dating and Marriage." One of the contributors stated, "Men are able to enjoy many of the benefits of marriage by living with a girlfriend without giving up their independence." [70] Here are some of the reasons men cited for not wanting to commit to marriage (according to the priority that the men gave them):

- They can get sex without marriage more easily than in times past.
- They can enjoy the benefits of having a wife by cohabiting rather than marrying.
- They fear that marriage will require too many changes and compromises.
- They are waiting for the perfect soul mate, and she hasn't yet appeared.
- They face few social pressures to marry, and they want to enjoy single life as long as they can. [71]

These things scream lack of commitment, a direct violation of Scripture. Ladies, is this the kind of man you want for a husband?

The National Marriage Project helpfully summarizes the problems with cohabitation:

> The primary way in which cohabitation differs in its social character from marriage is the lower level of interpersonal commitment that is involved, a phenomenon which surely is related to its more informal nature and to the absence of a formal promise or solemn pledge to stay together. Cohabiting partners tend to have a weaker sense of couple identity, less willingness to sacrifice for the other, and a lower desire to see the relationship go long term. This holds true even in nations where cohabitation has become common and institutionalized. One study using data from Norway and Sweden, for example, found that compared to married couples, cohabitors overall "are less serious, less satisfied, and more often consider to split up from their current relationships." [72]

Be wise and avoid this method. It's just a poorly made tool! And, by the way, you ought to be telling your friends as well to check out the research on this so they can see for themselves the significantly higher chance of divorce caused by living together before marriage.

Matching services that emphasize finding a "need meet-er"

Much of the secular (and even Evangelical) relationship literature emphasizes finding someone who will meet your needs. Whether the needs are for security, self-esteem, healing from past wounds, or something as mundane as enjoying the same hobbies, you are encouraged to find someone who will meet those needs.

Please hear me clearly: a relationship must have something deeper than "having needs met" to hold it together. Think about the word "needs" for a moment. Imagine a wife saying, "I need my husband to touch me more." Is she saying, "I need this like I need air to breathe" or is she saying, "I would really like to have this?" Some teach the right answer would be that her need has to be met. I believe though it is more like—"I really would like my husband to be more intimate" which is really saying, "I strongly desire my husband to be more intimate." This could then progress (or regress) to "I will not be happy unless he is touching me more." It ought to be obvious that this is more like lustful desires than legitimate God-given needs (like breathing). Wouldn't it be more biblical to say we can learn to be content in the Lord even when a spouse is disappointing us and not meeting our expectations or needs? The Lord desires to use these situations to help us grow in Christlikeness. That is a more biblical concept.

What happens when the one you married because he or she met some need in you, ceases to meet that need? What will you do when things change that were important to you when you were first married? For example, when Rose and I married, I was very interested in studying the history of the American Civil War and in collecting Civil War items. My "ideal marriage ceremony" was to have our wedding outside, with the groomsmen wearing Civil War uniforms and the bridesmaids wearing Southern dresses, hoops and all (sounds miserable, doesn't it?). As I grew in my relationship with the Lord, I began to realize that this was more than a just mere hobby to me. It was rooted in a proud heart that desired (needed?) to be recognized as a Civil War expert. But now, I don't need the Civil War expertise to feel fulfilled or to be my identity.

What would have happened if I had married a woman who was just as interested in the Civil War as I was, or was at least willing to stroke my ego so that we could be happy? What if she didn't change with me as I lost my passionate interest in this area? Disappointment would certainly have resulted, because the reason she married me no longer existed.

A main proponent of this view seems to believe there are deep longings in your soul that you must have someone satisfy in order to have a successful marriage. While giving his own personal testimony he wrote, "I was in need of someone whose partnership would help me feel better about myself." [73] In another place he wrote, "In short, you have to be smarter in order to be quicker and wiser. Being smarter involves a deep understanding of who you are, and what you need from another person in order to be truly fulfilled...." [74]

Adding To and Taking Away

This thinking troubles me, and I conclude that it both adds to and takes away from Scripture. It adds to Scripture with an inaccurate view of human nature and takes away by having a naïve view of the same. I fear that this need-meeting is potentially just stroking another person's idolatry. To be clear on this, I do not believe it is wrong to use a matching service. You just need (using the word correctly) to use it wisely, understanding there could be a Biblically inaccurate theory about human nature behind these services.

Traditional Dating

Dating in the United States is as common as baseball and football. It is the main methodology used now (along with cohabitation) to build romantic relationships, at least since the early twentieth century. [75] Dating can be defined as a boy and a girl spending time together for the sake of enjoyment because there is some type of attraction. Often, the result is a more steady romantic relationship in which the couple display some level of commitment to each other. Sometimes this dating relationship leads to marriage.

Some people in Christian circles have raised objections to traditional dating; they believe that it is not a good way to find a spouse because it leads to too many dangers. While I agree with that concern, I do believe dating can be done in a godly way.

Adding To or Taking Away

There are ways that dating can add to or take away from God's Word. The main way is probably purity. When a young man takes away the purity of a girl, he is clearly taking away from Scripture! I agree with the critics of traditional dating that this system almost expects a certain degree of physical intimacy. Of course, dating doesn't have to include this but often it does.

The dating atmosphere, with its emphasis on developing emotional ties, when combined with our sinfulness, the immaturity of those dating and the pressures of culture, seems to lend itself to impurity. Much is done in the name of love that is nothing but selfishness. It ought to be clear by this point in the book that if physical intimacy is the foundation of a relationship, it can cause structural weakness in the rest of the marriage house. So, if maintaining purity is a struggle for you, then this is not the best approach for developing a romantic relationship (see Romans 13:14).

Another key area in which traditional dating can fall short is in lack of parental involvement. Often, the parents have little to say in the romantic life of their teen because they either don't want to be involved, or don't realize they have the authority to be involved or they are too intimidated to be involved. Scripture is clear that children must obey and honor their father and mother, and that fathers are responsible to rear their children for the Lord (Ephesians 6:1). Your parents should be very involved in your romantic interests because there is so much potential for harm.

It is also clear that traditional dating does not meet the standards of Scripture when you get involved in relationships with an out-of-balance sense of need. For instance, a boy feels that he must have someone of the opposite sex like him. He enjoys being liked, and because of this view of human relationships, he takes an interest in just about anyone who seems to like him.

If you feel needy for a relationship with the opposite sex, please understand that it will be easy for you to turn that relationship into something God never intended. You should never become involved in a romantic relationship until you accept that your chief relationship is with the Lord. You must have a realistic view of other people. No other person can perfectly meet your "needs."

I wish someone had discipled me with these principles before I dated. Because of this, I desire to disciple my children and I do not want my children to date as I did. It needs to be better regulated and have clearer purposes, and my children need to be better prepared than I was before considering getting involved in a romantic relationship through dating. In summary, I can see the advantages of traditional dating (like enjoying getting to know someone); therefore, if you can date and not violate biblical principles, then this approach cannot be condemned. [76]

Betrothal

For many readers this next section will sound strange since an arranged marriage is not a common practice in Western cultures. Betrothal is the method by which the parents of the woman and the man agree that the couple should marry, and together the parents arrange the marriage. If this is the custom of your culture, you know better than I that your parents may not even allow you to have any opinion in the choice of your spouse. [77]

Betrothal has many supporters worldwide, even in the United States, because some believe that Scripture teaches this method above all others. Proponents of this method use India as the example to follow in the United States, and they point to the low divorce rate there as evidence of how well it works.

Adding To or Taking Away

The literature concerning betrothal teaches that young people will be protected from making bad marriages, and there can be no chance for divorce. However, what will happen when a couple who was married by this method experiences problems in their marriage, and divorce does occur? They will become disillusioned, and they will wonder what happened since they faithfully trusted their parents.

The low divorce rate in India is used to show how well this method works, but what is not cited are the common and horrendous stories of how wives in India are mistreated or even killed if they are not pleasing to their husbands. Some young women commit suicide to escape the horrors of their arranged marriage.

Consider the cultures of the Middle East and the low view of the status of women. The husband is firmly in control of his wife, and she is almost viewed as property (in some countries she is viewed as property). This is contrary to the dignity woman are given in

Scripture and a direct violation of the biblical way a husband is to treat his wife (see 1 Peter 3:7).

Scripture does describe marriage by betrothal, and even describes us as being "betrothed" to our Savior (2 Corinthians 11:2). Most of the couples mentioned in the Bible were married in this way, but God had regulated it so that it was practiced in a godly way. This was the common method during that time, but I do not believe that today God intends that all marriages be arranged.

Consider the story of Ruth, whose marriage to Boaz was God's will. They became part of the line of our Savior, but their marriage was not through betrothal (Ruth 3). In all of the passages where betrothal is mentioned, there is no passage in which it is commanded. Even though betrothal was the means used in biblical cultures, I do not believe it can be proved that it is the only way of finding a spouse. If you are going to say this is the biblical method, then you need to include all parts of the process, such as paying for your bride with camels!

Some of you may have no option though, because you live in a country that practices betrothal. If so, then use this methodology, but let biblical wisdom guide the way in which it is done.

Courtship

Courtship involves the idea of serious or focused dating with one person for the purpose of considering marriage. Some have even called this idea "biblical dating." [78] It does seem that traditional dating can turn into this after the couple gets more serious about one another.

Courtship implies that a boy is pursuing a girl and will seek her favor by godly acts of serving her and by other beautiful means of winning her affection. Sounds pretty chivalrous doesn't it! This is usually after the guy asks the father or parents for permission to biblically date the girl.

Joshua Harris summarizes this view well:

> What is courtship? It's dating with a purpose. It's friendship plus possibility. It's romance chaperoned by wisdom. That's what I

mean by setting a clear course for romance. It's not without risk; it's simply a way to be careful with the other person's heart while opening up your lives together to God's joyful best. [79]

Adding To or Taking Away

The only way I can see the courtship approach as adding to or taking away from Scripture would be if someone promotes this as *the only* biblical way to pursue relationships. Again, the danger would be promoting a method over growing in biblical wisdom.

Wisdom over Methodology

Of all the methods mentioned so far, I see myself endorsing a view somewhere between traditional dating and courtship or biblical dating (but leaning toward courtship). But, I write as an American and my views certainly are not inspired Scripture. The emphasis though, needs to be on (among other things) finding a follower of Christ who has the character qualities and mature readiness that can result in a stable marriage. This would demonstrate that you are endeavoring to use godly discernment. Scripture emphasizes wisdom instead of techniques for doing things, and this is why biblical truth transcends culture and time.

Let me illustrate this point with a story from my early years in pastoral ministry. One of the churches where I served on the staff had a unique way of choosing new elders. If the board needed to replace two members, the elders would nominate three men they believed met the qualifications of an elder in 1 Timothy 3. If the men agreed to serve, each name would be placed inside a sealed envelope and the envelopes would be placed in a closed office. After a time of prayer the head elder would go into that office and pick two of the envelopes. They believed that those two men were God's chosen ones because God had made the decision by the drawing of lots. As a staff member this method bothered me because it did not have much biblical support; it seemed so mystical, and it could lead to pride.

After the men were chosen, they were introduced to the congregation where the men gave a testimony. During one of these testimonies the issue of pride was substantiated. From my perspective, one of the men just oozed with it. He spoke about how he had been specially chosen by God, and from the tone of his voice, it seemed that he was quite proud that the "hand of God" had chosen him.

As a lowly staff member I did not have much say about such a well-established practice. I eventually reconciled it in my mind by realizing that the method used did not matter as much as whether the candidates were biblically qualified. Any method used under those circumstances would still result in qualified leadership.

It is clear that different cultures use different methods for building relationships. These methods change throughout time, but biblical principles remain the same. What then, are some consistent biblical principles you can count on?

Parental Involvement

Some of you are not going to want to read this, but Scripture shows that ideally parents are to be involved in the lives of their children and should disciple and mentor them, especially until they establish their own homes. Parents should remain a godly influence throughout their children's lives. Ephesians 6:4 calls fathers to bring up their children "in the nurture and admonition of the Lord." I'm sure many of you have experienced less than the ideal in your home, but in God's plan, the relationship between even an older child and parent should be so solid that you would want to seek godly input from your parents.

According to Scripture a father is responsible for whom he gives his daughter to in marriage. 1 Corinthians 7:38 says, "He who gives his own virgin daughter in marriage does well...." Scripture also teaches that a son leaves father and mother and cleaves to his wife, but a daughter is given in marriage. I'm sure you see the basis of this tradition in some marriage ceremonies where a father walks his daughter down the aisle and "gives her away." Matthew 24:38 says that in the last days everything will appear normal before the Lord returns since normal routines like marriage will take place. "They were marrying and giving in marriage...." For our purposes it is significant to note the twofold phrase—"marrying and giving in marriage." As Douglas Wilson has pointed out, "Sons *leave*, daughters are *given*." [80]

Ideally, a loving parent is discipling a child to make wise choices so that this very important decision does not happen haphazardly or based upon feelings. Parents also help protect purity (since desires are so strong). Even if you don't have godly parents, I would still urge you to weigh carefully the input of a parent, since your mother or father probably knows you better than any other person does. Another suggestion would be for you to get some good input from a spiritual parent, perhaps an older godly parent in your church who may serve as a mentor for you.

In our home these topics were regularly discussed, both in our family devotions and with each child individually. We prayed regularly for the yet unknown spouses of our children. We also had an agreement with our girls: if a guy would express an interest in her by asking her out on a date or something similar, he would need to talk with me. I actually had my daughters make this agreement with me, and we would shake hands on it! If they weren't really interested in the guy, then they would just express that kindly, but if they were interested they would have him talk with me. Because we trust our daughters, we were very careful to hear their desires through this process.

For some of you that sounds like too much parental involvement, but please remember the principle that a godly man "leads, provides for and protects." So it is my responsibility to help protect my daughters from unworthy men and to help give my sons guidance in choosing godly women, just as Solomon did with his son in Proverbs.

If parents don't agree with choices

This brings us to the painful topic of what to do when your parents disagree with your choice of someone to date or marry. I've seen a great deal of pain come from this scenario. I would beg you to proceed carefully and work hard at disciplining your emotions since you will be making decisions that can cause great harm and may have damaging effects for years.

Scripture makes it clear that you are to obey and honor your parents. [81] You knew I was going to start here, didn't you? Some questions probably pop into your mind. When I'm away at college, do I need to follow these verses? Is it ever okay to disobey my parents? Or, how about this one: do I need to live in a perpetual state of obedience until the time of my wedding? What if my parents disagree with my choice of the one I want to marry?

These verses teach that *children* are always under obligation to obey, but as *adults* they are commanded to always honor. Now, how does this work out in answering these questions?

I've been involved with a number of similar scenarios in recent years where parents disagree with their child's choice and in one case even refused to attend the wedding. In two of the situations the singles involved were independent adults, fully supporting themselves. Both sets of parents had the perspective that their son or daughter was required to obey them right up to the time of the wedding. What do you do?

The first question I believe you have to answer is, are you still a child or are you an adult? In chapter 7, on how you know when you're ready to get married, we defined maturing manhood and womanhood. In that chapter we saw that maturity involves things like providing for yourself. In other words, adults feed themselves; children have to be provided for. Can you see how this applies even when you are away at college? I know that you are in transition, but who is paying your bills? If you want to be treated like an adult by your parents, then it would be good to demonstrate adulthood. This doesn't mean your parents are totally correct in all they are saying, but if they are paying your bills, the command still applies with one exception.

The exception is that all human authority is limited if that authority is asking us to sin by disobeying a direct command of the Lord. A great example of this is found in Acts 5, where the Lord had given the apostles a clear command to preach the gospel, but the authorities were telling them to stop. Peter said, "We must obey God rather than man" (v. 29). It would be easy to abuse this principle, so you have to be honest with yourself and decide if what your parents are asking you to do is truly sin. Are they asking you to disobey a clear biblical command? Because your emotions are probably already stirred up at this point you should ask some older, godly believers to help you think through this question clearly.

Next, you are always to honor your parents. This would mean that even if you disagree with their opinion, you must be careful how you express it. If you disagree, the biblical way is to appeal calmly to your parents instead of yelling at them or closing yourself off from them. [82]

In the two cases I mentioned, it was determined by counselors that the singles involved were adults who were not obligated to obey their parents' wishes. We counseled each child how to appeal respectfully to the parents, but in the end the parents still objected. However, we advised the couple after a lot of prayer and other counsel using biblical principles, to go ahead and marry the person. As you can imagine, this was extremely painful, since in one case, the parents refused to come to the wedding. As I said before, walk very carefully when dealing with this kind of situation.

Purity Internally and Externally

We've already explored purity numerous times, but for the sake of thoroughness I'll just mention again that part of your methodology must be remaining sexually pure. Instead of asking, "How far can we go?" ask, "How pure do I want to be when I'm married?" You may say, "Well, it's too late for that!" Remember, though, that we believe in grace, and it's never too late to start doing what is right.

Preparation

While you are waiting for the Lord's timing for your marriage, you should be preparing yourself. Instead of asking yourself, "Who is the best fit for me?" ask, "Am I the right kind of person?" Do you have the skills that will make you a godly wife or a godly husband? Do you know the proper roles for such a wife or husband?

Wisdom tells you to start getting ready now, and when you do have a relationship, you can practice what you have been learning. As you grow, don't be surprised if the kind of person you are attracted to changes also!

Prayer and Patience

Prayer and patience are inextricably linked to each other. Prayer is the action that shows that we are dependent upon the Lord. Patience comes as we seek his guidance and determine to trust him. Psalm 27 puts both of these together. In verse 11 David prays, "Teach me Your way, O LORD, and lead me in a level path." In verse 14 he writes, "Wait for the LORD; be strong, and let your heart take courage; Yes, wait for the LORD." Be in prayer continually for God to supply the right mate, and be patient until he does by choosing to trust him.

Purpose

Be committed to relationships that have clear biblical purposes. I hope you have fun with members of the opposite sex but when it comes to romantic relationships, I hope you are focused on more than just that. This would include, among other things, approaching the relationship as an act of worship to the Lord (I Corinthians 10:31) and determining to honor and serve the other person (Philippians 2:1-12). Honoring and serving the other person would include breaking off the relationship as soon as you realize it is not wise. This is the loving thing to do.

People and Places

"He who walks with wise men will be wise. But the companion of fools will suffer harm" (Proverbs 13:20). It is wise to spend time in the right kinds of places and with the right kinds of people.

We've already emphasized the local church, but allow me to state the obvious again. What better place than in your own local church to find a spouse? This would indicate you have similar beliefs and possibly have been discipled by the same types of people.

Here are two more ideas: Mission trips are another place to find people who may share your biblical value system. Then there is always the obvious environment of friends at school who are part of the same Christian campus groups.

Just a reminder, as you are enjoying your friendships, and find yourself attracted to someone, please remember the principles of the heart that we learned in chapter 3. I can guarantee that your heart has more influence in your life than you realize.

Proper Questions

Through the years, as I've done premarital counseling, I've been amazed at how many couples did not know how their future spouse came to faith in Christ. This tells me that there is some degree of superficiality to the relationship. I hope that while you are enjoying getting to know one another you will be sure to talk about substantial things as well.

These questions could explore areas like, what are his or her values, talents, motivations, goals, desires, future plans, relationships, and Christian beliefs? Are you headed in the same direction in life? I urge you to do this because I am hoping this person will bless and not grieve your heart. Instead of breaking your heart I am hoping this person will strengthen it.

Whatever tool or method you use to build future relationships, it should include using the biblical principles stated above. They will make your tools effective.

To this day I remember that hot day digging the long trench by hand, and I still wonder why my father didn't use a backhoe.

Starting to prepare now:

1. What older person could serve as a mentor for you?

2. Is there a particular methodology that you have been taught is *the* way to find a spouse? Does it add to or take away from Scripture?

3. What is your attitude toward your parents? Is there something that you need to do to improve your relationship with them?

4. What would wisdom-in-action look like using one of the legitimate methodologies of your culture?

5. In what ways are you meeting (or not meeting) the requirements of being an adult?

6. How could your local church be involved in helping guide you?

7. What initial questions should you be asking yourself if you find yourself attracted to someone?

Part Three
The Roof

In **Part One** we answered ways to lay a solid foundation.

In **Part Two** we answered five key questions.

In **Part Three** we will answer "What will be the result of building wisely as an act of worship?"

Chapter 10

THE RESULT OF BUILDING WISELY

(A Marriage That Glorifies God)

> Whether, then, you eat or drink or whatever you do, do
> all to the glory of God.
>
> 1 Corinthians 10:31

When building a house, I always looked forward to the day we shingled the roof. One of my jobs was to carry the shingles up onto the roof. With great pride and attempted agility I would endeavor to walk up a ladder while balancing a bundle of shingles on each shoulder. Try to picture it: walking up the ladder without holding on! If you've ever known someone who does roofing or seen it being done, you know it's a very hot and dirty job. So why did I like it so much? Well, it definitely showed that progress was being made on the house, and as we did the shingling we could clearly see what was done and what still needed to be done. We always felt a sense of urgency as well, both to see how much we could get done in a day and to protect the house in case of rain. Most importantly, as we will discuss in this chapter, it gave the house a crowning touch.

Living for the Glory of God

No house is complete until it has a sturdy and attractive roof to crown the whole building project. According to Scriptural thinking, the roof that crowns your marriage house will be the glory of God. This will happen naturally as you obey the wise principles of God's Word, because obedience, with a motive of worship, always brings glory to God. Obedience to the wise principles of marriage preparation will change your life, and this change glorifies the Lord. 1 Corinthians 10:31 tells us, "Whether, then, you eat or drink or whatever you do, do all to the glory of God." We are called to glorify God in all we do, even the little things. If it is true for the small things, it is certainly true for marriage preparation, because it is the second most important decision in your life.

Just as the roof of a home points to the sky, it is my desire that your marriage point to heaven in praise to God. As you apply these principles to your life, the principle of sowing and reaping that is found many times in Scripture will take effect. Galatians 6:7 says, "Do not be deceived, God is not mocked; for whatever a man sows, this he will also reap." It's as blunt as this: whatever you have put into marriage preparation is what you will experience in your future marriage.

Paul goes on to warn us in the next verse, "For the one who sows to his own flesh shall from the flesh reap corruption" (Gal. 6 :8). This tells me that if you follow the natural desires of your heart, you will reap a weak marriage house. The bad fruit being seen in marriages today is a constant reminder that most sow to the flesh. However, I think you want something better, and you can have it!

Do you remember Proverbs 24:3-4? "By wisdom a house is built, and by understanding it is established; and by knowledge the rooms are filled with all precious and pleasant riches." The principle of sowing and reaping is also clearly evident here, and it ought to give you great hope for your future marriage. If you prepare by building your house wisely, then you can enjoy "rooms filled with all precious and pleasant riches." If you approach marriage with understanding, you can establish a firm or solid home that glorifies the Lord. This wisdom even helps us be realistic. Marriages will not be perfect because of the impact of Genesis 3 on our relationships. But, they will be incredibly more stable than those of our surrounding culture. What a great reassurance this gives in an age of divorce and dissatisfaction!

Living as Worshipers

What we're really saying when we say "live for the glory of God" is that we are to live as worshipers. Throughout the book I have been trying to emphasize preparing for marriage God's way, the wisdom way, and at the center of this is what I would call, living as a worshiper. As we saw in chapter 3, all of mankind worships someone or something. So, as we conclude this study together, let me make as clear as possible what I mean by living as a worshiper, which results in a God glorifying marriage, not perfect, but definitely stable and honoring to God.

The apostle Paul wrote one of the grandest doxologies of Scripture right at the hinge point of the book of Romans. He said, "Oh, the depth of the riches both of the wisdom and knowledge of God! How unsearchable are His judgments and unfathomable His ways!" He is extolling the great virtues of our Sovereign Lord as he revels in the wonders of having just written eleven chapters concerning God's redemptive plan for history. Paul then helps us to understand what it means to live daily in light of the greatness of this God: "For *from* Him and *through* Him and *to* Him are all things. To Him be the glory forever. Amen" (Romans 11:36) [emphasis added]. He then begins chapter 12 through the end of the book telling us how this manifests itself in our lives, which is our "spiritual service of worship" (12:1). The last chapters are full of practical applications about how to live as a worshiper because of the gospel; in relationship to each other, to the government, and when inevitable controversy occurs.

Worship and Your Future Marriage

How does this thinking apply to your personal marriage preparation and your future marriage? Here it is: live in preparation for marriage as if everything is from him, through him and to him. Then live out your marriage as if it is from, through and to him.

In other words, your future spouse will be *from* him. Live choosing to believe this instead of worrying or manipulating your circumstances to get what you want. Everything comes through the hand of God first before entering into your life. Will you believe it? Then, after you're married, live believing this person came from the Lord. That truth will serve you when things aren't going well in your marriage.

Then live wisely, preparing for marriage *through* the Lord. It is difficult and may seem overwhelming, but building a house is always hard work. He promises though, "[You] can do all things through Him who strengthens [you]" (Philippians 4:13). Will you choose to believe that your Sovereign Lord, who cares very much about you and your future marriage, will strengthen you? As you answer the questions at the end of the chapters and endeavor to make changes that will help you make wiser choices and be better prepared, believe he wants to help you.

Finally, do all of this *to* (unto) the Lord. As you are endeavoring to grow, tell the Lord, "I'm doing this because I believe this is what you want me to do." And then when you are married, love your spouse as an act of worship to the Lord.

All of life can be lived this way: paying bills, doing school work, doing your job, and eventually raising children. What an exciting way to live as we learn to live all of life as worship!

Reviewing the Building Plan

Let's briefly review all of the sections of our house. In Part One, we poured a solid foundation by emphasizing the importance of biblical wisdom and building your life on Christ as one of his followers. We also established the importance of knowing why God designed marriage so that you may marry for the right reasons and find another person who has the same motivations. In the last part of the foundation section we studied heart desires and why you are attracted to certain people. This understanding is crucial so that you will become wiser about yourself and work on finding your chief satisfaction in him.

In Part Two, we built the first floor. Each of these chapters contain principles to strengthen the walls of your future marriage relationship. We started by exploring how to have the right focus during your single years. Instead of focusing on finding a husband or wife, focus on becoming who the Lord would want you to be. The next room added was to consider how important it is to start *now*; you need to be building good relationship character traits and skills into your life. In particular, you should be working on communication and conflict resolution skills with people like siblings, parents, roommates and coworkers. Chapter 7 led you to think about the biblical answer to the question, "How will I know when I'm ready for marriage?" The answer—when you are seeing displayed in your life the characteristics of a maturing man or woman. As we continued to build, a very logical question was raised, "How will I know God's will?" In chapter 8 you were encouraged to do what you know God wants you to do (start getting yourself ready) and trust him, as your shepherd, to do his part (giving you wisdom and leading you to the right person). Then, in chapter 9 we saw that both having the proper perspective on methods and also following the proper pattern leads to choosing someone wisely. When you put it all together, it looks like Figure 4.

If you and your future partner commit yourself to these principles, you can have a custom-built home made by none other than the Designer of the universe. You will then be ready for a certificate of occupancy. As you build—keep submitting your potential home to the ultimate building inspector to evaluate your progress. Allow him to keep checking and adjusting your desires so your home will truly bring glory to him and you will reap the benefits.

When a home is complete, someone has to go through the home and check to make sure everything is working properly and meets the new owner's approval. When something is not correct, it gets noted on a "punch list" (I don't know why it's called that) so that it can be corrected. Let's go through a basic checklist to check to see if you pass inspection, if you don't, make your own "punch list" of things you need to correct.

Figure 4

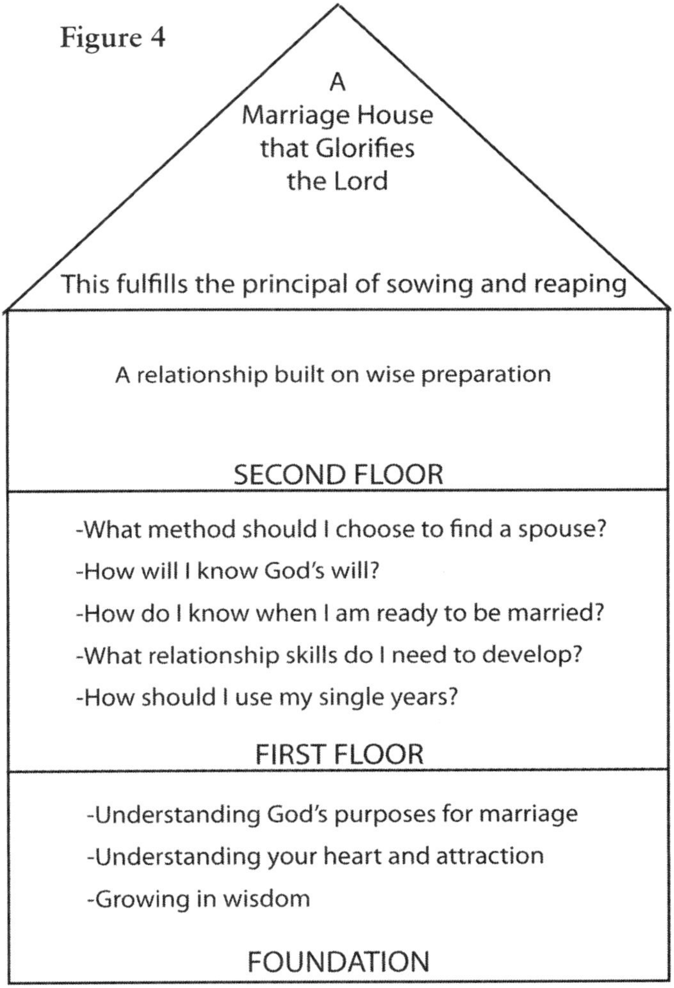

A
Marriage House
that Glorifies
the Lord

This fulfills the principal of sowing and reaping

A relationship built on wise preparation

SECOND FLOOR

-What method should I choose to find a spouse?

-How will I know God's will?

-How do I know when I am ready to be married?

-What relationship skills do I need to develop?

-How should I use my single years?

FIRST FLOOR

-Understanding God's purposes for marriage

-Understanding your heart and attraction

-Growing in wisdom

FOUNDATION

"Unless the LORD build the house, they labor in vain who build it."

-Psalm 127:1

"By wisdom a house id built and by understanding it is established; and by knowledge the rooms are filled with all precious and pleasant riches."

-Proverbs 24:3-4

Building checklist (the same checklist could be used for determining what you should be looking for in another person):

Rate yourself on a scale of 1-4 with 1 being low and 4 being high.

___1. I am committed to pursuing biblical wisdom.

___2. I am committed to the Lordship of Christ and committed to his Lordship over my relationships.

___3. I am committed to God's stated purposes for marriage.

___4. I am growing in my own heart awareness so that I have a better understanding of my desires and attractions—what I have been and should be worshiping.

___5. I desire to use my single years wisely, which means I am committed to a good local church.

___6. I have started to work on the key relationship skills of conflict resolution and communication in my current relationships, and I understand that I should not wait until I am in a serious relationship to do so.

___7. I understand that marriage is for the mature, so I am willing to work on becoming a godly man or godly woman with the responsibilities that involves.

___8. I am committed to asking good questions based on biblical convictions about any person I am interested in, seeking God's will, but not seeking his will through special signs or through feelings.

___9. I am committed to using biblical wisdom in whatever methods my culture promotes.

___10. I desire to live as a worshiper of the true and living God so that I can reap the benefits of living by his principles.

Starting to prepare now:

1.   As you look over the building checklist, which two do you need to work on the most? How will you do it?

2.   Based upon what you have learned about marriage, wisdom, yourself, and relationships, write a concluding prayer of commitment to the Lord.

Appendix 1

The Psalm 18 Study

Read Psalm 18:1-3. Read the explanations given below for each of the metaphors used to describe God. Be thorough as you answer the questions following the metaphors.

Warning! You'll want to answer God or Jesus for the questions. Please be honest, is he really the answer all the time as your *first* or regular, normal response to the pressures of life?

Verse One: **Strength**—to bind fast, to give support, like a retaining wall or buttress. This was used 34 times in Nehemiah for giving support to the walls of Jerusalem as they were rebuilt. David describes God as his strength, his support, his buttress.

1) *Question*: What is my support? What do I rely on to make me strong? What gives me strength to go through life? What do I lean upon when life is tough? To whom do I turn?

Verse Two:

Rock—also translated as cliff, a place to hide.

2) *Question*: In what do I hide? Where do I find shelter? From what do I derive comfort?

Fortress: stronghold, a castle on a mountain. David flees to the Lord as his fortress; he takes refuge from the pressures of life in him.

3) *Question*: To whom or to what do I typically flee in the storms of life? What is my refuge?

Deliverer: the One who helps me escape, used of survivors from battle.

4) *Question:* To whom or to what am I turning for help in

escaping the pressures and the battles of life? What are my escapes?

Rock: This is different from the preceding use of the word "rock." In Psalm 62:1-3, Rock is used for the people who are confident because their faith and trust are in the Lord; therefore, they will not be "greatly shaken."

5) *Question*: In whom or what is my confidence placed? Do I believe it will keep me from being greatly shaken?

Shield: small, maneuverable shield. (See Psalm 28:7 for full body shield.)

6) *Question*: What are my shields in life? What am I hiding behind? Who or what am I trusting to protect me? What are my defense mechanisms?

Horn of my salvation: the figure of one clinging to the horns of the altar as a refuge for forgiveness; a horn used in battle.

7) *Question*: What do I cling to when I am attacked? What would victory look like to me? What would win the battle for me so that I can have peace? What is my salvation? What makes life livable? What do I turn to as a weapon to win peace in my life?

Stronghold: fort.

8) *Question*: What walls do I hide behind? In what do I bury myself? What do I immerse myself in when the pressure is on?

Verse Three: "And I am saved from my enemies."

9) *Question*: What is causing pressure? Am I doing what David did under pressure? What are the giants or enemies in my life (people, emotions, habits)?

David says that God is all things to him. What am I allowing to take God's rightful place?

Do I devote more devotion, zeal, energy, or passion to these things than to my relationship with the Lord?

What can I do to put the Lord in his rightful place?

What thoughts do I need to change?

What verses should I memorize to help my thinking?

What could you do to make the Lord your ROCK tangibly?

What would demonstrate that? What would hiding behind him as your shield look like in real life?

Appendix 2

Marriage Preparation Project

Instructions: The goal of this project is to help you prepare for your future marriage (even if you are not currently in a romantic relationship) and to have healthier, God-glorifying relationships in general. I believe that Scripture can help you discern why you relate to others in the way that you do, and it can give you guidance to change in a way that not only glorifies the Lord but also encourages you. However, you need to be willing to do some work. As Paul said, "Discipline yourself for the purpose of godliness" (1 Timothy 4:7). But be encouraged because the Lord says as you learn the truth, the truth can set you free (John 8: 31-32).

Ideally, even though I think it is possible for you to do this on your own, it is far superior to have a mentor or discipler help you. This person can be praying for you and also hold you accountable to work on the areas you need to change. As you answer the questions and develop a Scriptural plan, that mentor may also be able to help you recognize things you weren't seeing on your own.

For the purposes of this project the assumption is that you are a follower of the Lord. If that is not the way you would describe yourself, then please go back and review chapter 2 before endeavoring to do this project.

Step 1: Pray and commit this project to the Lord. Ask the Lord to help you to be teachable and ask the Holy Spirit to change you.

Step 2: Because this project is based upon the questions at the end of chapter 3 and the diagram in chapter 6, you will need to go back and answer the questions at the end of those chapters. Please refresh your memory on the contents of chapters 3 and 6.

The questions about the heart from chapter 3 and the diagram from chapter 6 are at the end of this appendix as well.

Step 3: After you have reread the section at the end of chapter 3 that gives examples of possible heart themes, and based upon how you answered the questions, ask yourself which best represents what your heart worships. It would be helpful to have your parents or a mentor help you come to some conclusions. You may not see your particular struggle on my list but maybe my list triggers your thinking.

What would you call the tendencies of your inner person? What do you tend to serve? According to the definitions of the heart given in chapter 3, your heart is the immaterial part of your being consisting of your mind, will, and emotions. Your desires also tell you a lot about your heart. So what do your thinking, emotions, and decisions reveal about what you desire? For the purposes of this project please pick only one heart issue, even though you may sense more than one operating in your desires. Which one seems to cause the most negative fruit in your life?

The list of potential heart issues is at the end of this appendix as well. The Psalm 18 study in Appendix 1 may also help you see what functionally have become the rocks and refuges in your life in the place of God.

Step 4: Review the list of character traits from chapter 6. As you think about the definitions given, evaluate yourself. Another way to do this would be to think of the opposites of each of these character traits and how they influence relationships. As we saw in chapter 6, it is the opposites of these character traits that can destroy relationships. For example, the opposite of gentleness would be harshness. Living with a harsh person can be very difficult and can deeply impact a relationship. Pick the one character trait you need to work on the most.

1. Compassion
2. Kindness
3. Humility
4. Gentleness
5. Patience
6. Bearing with one another
7. Forgiveness
8. Love

Step 5: Review the list of relationship skills. Which one do you need to work on the most?

- Communication skills: staying current with one another and just talking about life together.
- Conflict resolution skills: knowing how to bring conflicts to resolution.
- Understanding roles: knowing who does what and why in the relationship.
- Worship: common religious beliefs, heading in the same direction spiritually and walking with the Lord together.
- Time together: for healthy relationships time must be invested.
- Honoring and serving one another: doing nice things for each other with an attitude of respect.

Step 6: Now, look at the triangle (reproduced here from chapter 6) and ask yourself how this heart theme influences your relationship skills and character traits. For example, if control is a desire of your heart, how does that impact the way you talk with others? Or, if you tend to be a people pleaser, how does that influence the way you deal with conflict? Analyze each of the other character traits as well. It would be wise to also ask yourself, "What could happen in my future marriage if my heart, relationship skills, and character traits do not change?" Write out the answers to these questions.

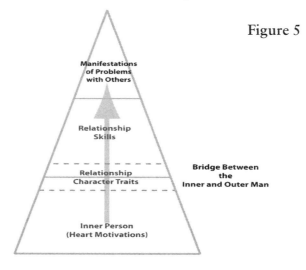

Figure 5

Step 7: A Plan for Change

The gospel makes it possible to change and become more like our Savior. I'm thankful that I'm not stuck with my weak relationship skills and character traits. The Lord desires to change us so we can live reflecting more glory to him.

As you begin to see how the bottom level of the triangle (your heart) influences the next level above it (relationship skills and character traits), ask yourself what is the one relationship skill or one character trait you need to work on the most. Maybe you've begun to see that there is more than one major heart theme. As I said before, focus on the one that seems to be the most dominant, having the most negative impact on your relationship skills and character traits. Now answer the following questions to come up with a plan for change.

1. In what ways does the gospel influence how you should think about relationships? How would aspects of the gospel like forgiveness, grace, and mercy impact the way you interact with others?

2. What is the opposite of the negative heart issue you have chosen to work on? For example, if desiring to be in control of your circumstances is the heart issue, then the opposite biblically would be to worship the Lord for his sovereignty (see Isaiah 40-48). How could you do this throughout the day?

3. What do you need to be thinking about? What do you need to meditate on?

4. What decisions need to be made?

5. What do your emotions reveal about the attitudes of your heart?

6. How could you grow in your love of the Lord and others? The two great commandments directly address the tendencies of the inner person to love the wrong things (see Matthew 22: 36-40). How could you work on loving the Lord more than these desires? How could you work on loving others more by working on proper relationship skills and character traits? Please try to think practically in terms of things you could do daily or regularly.

7. What would the answers to these questions look like in action as you drive to work? As you walk to classes? As you interact with roommates and friends? As you interact with your parents?

8. What would be some practical things to work on daily and weekly for that one relationship skill or character trait?

9. What verses could you meditate on or memorize that directly applies to your plan?

10. Based upon the answers to these questions, what have you learned about yourself, your evaluation of your character traits and relationship skills; and keeping the flow of thought of the diagram in mind, prayerfully make a list of things to do daily/regularly to carry out your plan. If you need motivation to do this please remember that you're doing this for the Lord and for your future spouse. Working on these areas now will make your future marriage stronger and help you choose a spouse wisely.

Step 8: Why not pray right now and commit this whole project to the Lord, and then ask a parent or mentor to hold you accountable for carrying out your plan.

Chapter 3 Questions:

1. When do you tend to experience fear, worry, or anxiety? (Matthew 19:34).

2. In what area have you struggled with disappointment? (Proverbs 13:12, 19).

3. In what situations do you struggle with anger? (James 4:1, 2; Proverbs 11:23).

4. Where do you encounter problems in relationships? (James 4:1-10).

5. What life situations do you find particularly difficult ? (1 Corinthians 10:13, 14).

6. What kinds of things do you find yourself trying to avoid?

7. In what way have you experienced regular problems in your relationship with the Lord?

8. In what situations do you tend to doubt the truths of Scripture?

9. What is a good relationship? What do you expect of others?

10. In what type of situations do you struggle with bitterness?

11. When have you struggled with regret, being tempted to say, "If only_____?

12. What experiences from the past do you have a hard time letting go?

13. In what area do you tend to struggle with envy? What do you find yourself wanting that others have?

14. Whose opinions really matter to you?

Adapted from The Journal of Biblical Counseling, Fall 1996

Possible heart/desire themes (Chapter 3):

1. **Control:** "I have to know the future to be happy." "Life is all right if my life is organized and I have it under control."

2. **Pleasure:** "Life is about having fun." "I need to hang around people who like to have fun." "The way to handle the pressures of life is by giving myself some pleasure."

3. **Keeping people happy:** "I am very concerned about what people think of me." "I have to make sure that I look good." "I must avoid conflicts." "There are some people that I am really afraid of."

4. **Success:** "I must be successful." "I am pursuing this degree because it will help me make a lot of money and make me look successful." "I must dress a certain way to look successful."

5. **Material things:** "The way to be happy is to be able to buy things." "It makes me feel good to shop."

6. **Money:** "I need money to be secure."

7. **Comfort:** "Life's about taking it easy and relaxing."

Notes

1. Leon Kass and Amy Kass, *Wing to Wing, Oar to Oar: Readings on Courting and Marrying,* The Ethics of Everyday Life (Notre Dame, Ind.: University of Notre Dame Press, 2000). The Introduction has an excellent analysis of how we have gotten to where we are in American culture related to marriage.
2. David Popenoe and Barbera Dafoe Whitehead, *The State of Our Unions 1999: The Social Health of Marriage in America* (Piscataway, N.J.: Rutgers, The State University of New Jersey, 1999), 4.
3. Ibid., 10
4. New American Standard Update
5. John N. Oswalt, "זוּכ," in *The Theological Wordbook of the Old Testament*, ed. R. Laird Harris, Gleason L. Archer, Jr., and Bruce K. Waltke (Chicago: Moody Press, 1980), 1:433.
6. Ibid., 434.
7. Charles Schmitz and Elizabeth Schmitz, "Debunking the Divorce Rate Myth," SelfGrowth.Com: The Online Self Improvement Community, accessed May 20, 2013, http://www.selfgrowth.com/articles/Debunking_The_Divorce_Rate_Myth.html.
8. Later in the book we will address the issue of whether you need to wait until you are older to marry, as current wisdom suggestions. I highlighted this section, though, because of their use of the term wisdom.
9. We will also discuss later the importance of the principle that a couple need to be headed in the same way spiritually and have the same convictions about the Lord.
10. Charles Schmitz and Elizabeth Schmitz, "Debunking the Divorce Rate Myth," SelfGrowth.Com: The Online Self Improvement Community, accessed May 20, 2013, http://www.selfgrowth.com/articles/Debunking_The_Divorce_Rate_Myth.html.
11. This is a typical Hebrew poetic device called parallelism.

12. D. R. W. Wood and I. H. Marshall, *New Bible Dictionary*, 3rd ed. (Leicester: InterVarsity Press, 1996).
13. Ibid.
14. Jack P. Lewis, "תעד," in *The Theological Wordbook of the Old Testament,* eds. R. Laird Harris, Gleason L. Archer, Jr., and Bruce K. Waltke (Chicago: Moody Press, 1980), 1:66.
15. The Hebrew word is "bĭn" and can simply mean "between."
16. David Beale, "The Rise and Fall of Harvard" in *Detroit Baptist Seminary Journal* 3, (1998): 91, accessed April 24, 2013, https://www.dbts.edu/journals/1998/beale.pdf.
17. The phrase "Genesis 3 hangover" originated with Dr. George Zemek at The Master's Seminary
18. David Powlison and John Yenchko, *Pre-engagement, 5 Questions to Ask Yourselves* (Phillipsburg, NJ: P&R Publishing, 2000), 3.
19. Ibid., 4
20. I heard this statement originally from Dr. Rick Holland while he was on staff at Grace Community Church.
21. Tom Lasswell and Marcia Lasswell, *Marriage and the Family* (Belmont, CA: Wadsworth Publishing Co., 1987), 56.
22. "Attraction," *Merriam-Webster*, accessed April 28, 2013, http://www.merriam-webster.com/dictionary/attraction?show=0&t=1405930422.
23. This theory teaches that because of "survival of the fittest" tendencies we are unconsciously looking for someone that will help our genes survive and thrive.
24. Harville Hendrix, *Getting the Love You Want* (New York: Henry Holt & Co., 1988), 36.
25. Andrew Bowling, "בבל," in *Theological Wordbook of the Old Testament* eds. R. Laird Harris, Gleason L. Archer, Jr., and Bruce K. Waltke (Chicago: Moody Press, 1980), 1:466.
26. "Thoughts" is a word that also means imaginations or ponderings. "Intentions" means our plans and insights. William F. Arndt and F. Wilbur Gingrich, eds., A Greek-English Lexicon of the New Testament and Other Early Christian Literature, 4th rev. ed. (Chicago: University of Chicago Press, 1952), 265-266.

27. See Appendix 1 for a full study on the metaphors in verses 1-3 and how they can help you determine what you truly worship.

28. Stuart Scott, *The Exemplary Husband: A Biblical Perspective* (Bemidji, Minn.: Focus Publishing, Inc., 2000), 103.

29. Augustine, *Confessions*, trans. Albert C. Outler, ed.Tom Gill (Gainesville, FL: Bridge-Logos, 2003), 11.

30. David H. Olson, John DeFrain, and Amy K. Olson, *Building Relationships: Developing Skills for Life* (Minneapolis: Life Innovations, Inc. 1999), 87

31. For example, see the annual "State of Our Unions" report published each year by the University of Virginia.

32. Janice Shaw Crouse, *Marriage Matters* (New Brunswick: Transaction Publishers, 2012), 118.

33. For example, think of how this couple could use their home as a way to minister to others.

34. The Hebrew of "not good for man to be alone" literally says, not good to be "by himself." I believe we have incorrectly read loneliness into it.

35. R. Laird Harris, Gleason Archer, Bruce Waltke, eds., *Theological Wordbook of the Old Testament* (Chicago: Moody Press, 1980), 1:47.

36. Ibid.

37. Much sociological evidence has been accumulated to reinforce that God's design for the family is what is best for children. For example, look at "The State of Our Unions" reports.

38. R. Laird Harris, Gleason Archer and Bruce Waltke, eds., *Theological Wordbook of the Old Testament,* (Chicago: Moody Press, 1980), 1:128

39. Ibid., 1:125. Also, read Genesis 15 to get an idea of the seriousness of this ceremony.

40. Jay E. Adams, *Marriage, Divorce and Remarriage According to the Bible* (Grand Rapids: Zondervan, 1980), 13

41. Ibid., 8.

42. The word "cleave" is even used about glue in Hebrew.

43. Jeffery S. Forrey,"Biblical Counsel for Concerned Singles" (*Journal of Biblical Counseling*, 14, no. 3 (1996): 24.

44. See the following article for a discussion of this. Stephen Vantas-
    sel, "Celibacy: The Forgotten Gift of the Holy Spirit." (Jo*urnal
    of Biblical Counseling* 12, no. 3 (1994): 20-23.
45. Ibid., 22.
46. Edward T. Welch, "Self Control: The Battle Against 'One More,'."
    Journal of Biblical Counseling 19, no. 2 (2001): 31.
47. Ibid., 31.
48. John Piper, and Wayne Grudem, eds. *Recovering Biblical Manhood
    & Womanhood: A Response to Evangelical Feminism* (Wheaton,
    Ill.: Crossway Books, Good News Publishers, 1991), 39.
49. David Popenoe, and Barbara Dafoe Whitehead, *The State of Our
    Unions 2003: The Social Health of Marriage in America* (Pis-
    cataway, N.J.: Rutgers, The State University of New Jersey,
    2001), 10.
50. The list in Colossians is more complete than the list in Ephesians.
51. All definitions are from, *A Greek English Lexicon of the New
    Testament* (William Arndt and F. Wilbur Gingrich)
52. If you find that you struggle with resentment I would urge you to
    read about the "Four Promises of Forgiveness" in *Peacemaking
    for Families* by Ken Sande.
53. John MacArthur, *The MacArthur New Testament Commentary,
    Commentary* on Matthew 1-7(Chicago: Moody Press, 1997),
    397-398.
54. In essence, I was introduced to these four communication prin-
    ciples by Dr. Jay Adams.
55. Please consider reading more on this topic from Peacemaker
    Ministries.
56. See the "PAUSE principle" from Peacemaker Ministries for a
    plan to follow that leads to resolving issues.
57. This diagram is from Dr. John Bettler, former Director of The
    Christian Counseling and Educational Foundation, during a
    Doctorate of Ministry class at Westminster Theological Semi-
    nary in the year 2000. I added the section on character traits.
58. Everett F. Harrison, ed. *Baker's Dictionary of Theology* (Grand
    Rapids: Baker Book House, 1960), 345.

59. John Piper, and Wayne Grudem, eds. *Recovering Biblical Manhood & Womanhood*, 33.

60. This definition is adapted from Chapter One of Recovering Biblical Manhood and Womanhood edited by John Piper and Wayne Grudem (Wheaton, Ill.: Crossway, 1991).

61. *Recovering Biblical Manhood and Womanhood* actually lists nine characteristics of servant leadership, but I selected these two since they seemed to be the two that a single man could work toward right away.

62. John Piper, and Wayne Grudem, eds. *Recovering Biblical Manhood & Womanhood*, 39.

63. The LORD's control over nature is also majestically proclaimed in verse 12 of the same chapter.

64. Jerry Bridges, *Trusting God, Even When Life Hurts* (Colorado Springs: NavPress, 1988), 200.

65. John MacArthur, *Reckless Faith, When the Church Loses Its Will to Discern* (Wheaton, Ill: Crossway Books, 1994), 223-224.

66. James C Petty, *Step by Step: Divine Guidance for Ordinary Christians* (Phillipsburg, NJ: P&R Publishing, 1999), 59.

67. Gary Friesen, and Robin J. Maxson, *Decision Making and the Will of God: A Biblical Alternative to the Traditional View* (Portland: Multonomah Press,1980), 303.

68. David Popenoe, and Barbera Dafoe Whitehead, *The State of Our Unions 2003*, 10.

69. It is interesting to note that e-Harmony alone had sales of $95 million in 2005 but that number increased to $275 million in 2012 according to privico.com

70. Barbara Dafoe Whitehead, interviewed in a press release for the "State of Our Unions 2002" from the National Marriage Project at Rutgers University, June 25, 2002. http://www.eurekalert.org/pub_releases/2002-06/rtsu-nrr062502.php#.

71. Ibid.

72. David Popenoe, "Cohabitation, Marriage and Child Wellbeing: A Cross-National Perspective." (Piscataway, NJ: National Marriage Project, 2008), 13. accessed September 12, 2014, http://

www.smartmarriages.com/uploaded/ Cohabitation.Report.
Popenoe. 08.pdf.

73. Neil Clark Warren, *How to Know If Someone Is Worth Pursuing in Two Dates or Less* (Nashville, Tenn.: Thomas Nelson Publishers, 1999), 19.

74. Ibid., 10.

75. Before this time it would have been the more traditional idea of courtship.

76. *Holding Hearts, Holding Hands* Sharon and Richard Phillips, (Phillipsburg, NJ: P& R Publishing, 2006). This is a great book to help you practice dating in a godly way.

77. If this is the case, then you must trust that your Lord is sovereignly fulfilling his plan for your life through your parents.

78. Douglas Wilson, *Her Hand in Marriage: Biblical Courtship in the Modern World* (Moscow, ID: Canon Press, 1997), 16.

79. Joshua Harris, *Boy Meets Girl: Say Hello to Courtship* (Sisters, Or.: Multnomah Publishers, 2005), 56.

80. Wilson, *Her Hand in Marriage*, 31

81. Ephesians 6:1-2

82. Ken Sande, *Peacemaking for Families* (Colorado Springs, CO: Focus on the Family, 2002) This is a wonderful resource on how to deal with family conflict and would give you thorough guidance on how to deal with a tense relationship with you parents in a godly way.

BIBLIOGRAPHY

Adams, Jay E. Marriage, *Divorce and Remarriage According to the Bible*. Grand Rapids: Zondervan Corporation, 1980.

Arndt, William F., and F. Wilbur Gingrich. 4th rev. aug. ed. *A Greek-English Lexicon of the New Testament and Other Early Christian Literature*. Chicago: University of Chicago Press, 1952.

Associated Press. Study links cohabitation before marriage, divorce. np. Online: http://www.wcinet.com/th/News/020399/National/143718.htm. August 24, 2000.

Boice, James Montgomery. *Genesis: An Expositional Commentary.* Vol. 1, Genesis 1:1-11:32. Grand Rapids: Zondervan Corporation, 1982.

Brenton, Sir Lancelot C.L. *The Septuagint Version: Greek and English*. Grand Rapids: Zondervan Publishing House, 1970.

Bridges, Jerry. *Trusting God, Even When Life Hurts.* Colorado Springs: NavPress, 1988.

Brown, Francis, ed. *The New Brown, Driver, and Briggs Hebrew and English Lexicon of the Old Testament.* Lafayette, Ind.: Book Publishers' Press, Inc., 1907.

Bullinger, E. W. *How to Enjoy the Bible: A Guide to Better Understanding and Enjoyment of God's Word.* Grand Rapids: Kregel Publications, 1990. Original edition, London: Eyre and Spottiswoode, 1916.

Castleberry, Stephen B., and Mrs.Stephen B. *Waiting for Her Isaac.* Poplar, Wis.: Castleberry Farms Press, 1997.

Clark, Jeramy. *I Gave Dating a Chance.* Colorado Springs: Waterbrook Press, Random House, Inc., 2000.

Crabb, Larry. *The Marriage Builder.* Grand Rapids: Zondervan Publishing House, 1992.

Davidson, Benjamin. *The Analytical Hebrew and Chaldee Lexicon.* Grand Rapids:Zondervan Publishing House, 1970.

Delitzsch, F. 1980. *Commentary on the Old Testament, Proverbs, Ecclesiastes, Song of solomon,* vol VI. Grand Rapids: William B. Eerdmans Publishing Company.

Doan, Eleanor, comp. *The Speaker's Sourcebook of 4000 Illustrations, Quotations, Sayings, Anecdotes, Poems, Attention-Getter, Sentence-Sermons, etc.* Grand Rapids: Zondervan Publishing House, 1960.

Edersheim, Alfred, D.D. Ph. D. *The Life and Times of Jesus the Messiah.* Vol. 1. Grand Rapids: Wm. B. Eerdmans Publishing Company, 1950.

E/harmony. Home Page. np. Online: http://www. eharmony.com/core/eharmony?cmd=eh-different. October15, 2002.

Elliot, Elisabeth. *Passion and Purity: Learning to Bring Your Love Life Under Christ's Control.* Grand Rapids: Fleming H. Revell, Baker Book House, 1984.

Eyrich, Howard, A. *Three to Get Ready: A Christian Premarital Counseling Manual.* Grand Rapids: Baker Book House, 1978.

Forrey, Jeffery S. "Biblical Counsel for Concerned Singles." *The Journal of Biblical Counseling* 14, no. 3 (1996): 24-32.

Friesen, Garry, and J. Robin Maxson. *Decision Making & the Will of God: A Biblical Alternative to the Traditional View.* Portland: Multnomah Press, 1980.

Gallagher, Maggie. "Where Have All the Grownups Gone?" *Family Policy* 13, Family Research Council, (2000): 1-4.

Godet, Frederic Louis. *Commentary on First Corinthians.* Grand Rapids: Kregel Publications, 1977. Original edition, Edinburgh: T. & T. Clark, 1889 under *Commentary on St. Paul's First Epistle to the Corinthians.*

Harris, Joshua. *I Kissed Dating Goodbye.* Sisters, Ore.: Multnomah Publishers, Inc., 1997.

———. *Boy Meets Girl: Say Hello to Courtship.* Sisters, Ore.: Multnomah Publishers, Inc., 2000.

Harris, R. Laird, ed. *Theological Wordbook of the Old Testament.* Vol. 1. Chicago: Moody Press, 1980.

———. *Theological Wordbook of the Old Testament.* Vol. 2. Chicago: Moody Press, 1980.

Harrison, Everett F., ed. *Baker's Dictionary of Theology.* Grand Rapids: Baker Book House, 1960.

Holland, Rick. *A Roadmap For Righteous Relationships: Biblical Directions for Finding Your Way.* Sun Valley, Calif.: Grace Community Church, 1999. 8 cassettes.

Jones, Debby and Jackie Kendall. *Lady in Waiting: Developing your Love Relationships.* Shippensburg, Pa.: Destiny Image Publishers, Inc., 1995.

Kass, Amy A. and Leon R. Kass, ed. *Wing to Wing, Oar to Oar: Readings on Courting and Marrying.* Notre Dame, Ind.: University of Notre Dame Press, 2000.

Keil, C. F., and F. Delitzsch. *Commentary on the Old Testament in Ten Volumes,* Vol. 4. Grand Rapids: William B. Eerdmans Publishing Company, 1980.

Kidner, Derek, Rev. *The Proverbs: An Introduction and Commentary.* Downers Grove, Ill.: InterVarsity Press, 1964.

King, Clayton, and Charie.King. *12 Questions to Ask Before You Marry.* Eugene, OR: Harvest House, 2011.

Kirby, Theresa M, ed. Press Release State of Our Unions. Rutgers University. Online: marriageproject@email. rutgers.edu., June 26, 2002.

Kittel, Gerhard, ed. *Theological Dictionary of the New Testament.* Vol. 1. Grand Rapids: William B. Eerdmans Publishing Company, 1964.

Lawson, George. *Proverbs: Timeless Truths for Practical Living.* Grand Rapids: Kregel Publications, 1980.

Lenski, R. C. H. *The Interpretation of St. Paul's First and Second Epistles to the Corinthians.* Minneapolis: Augsburg Publishing House, 1963.

Leupold, H. C., D.D. *Exposition of Genesis: Vol. 1,* Chap. 1-19. Grand Rapids:Baker Book House, 1942.

Lindvall, Jonathan. Dating? Courtship? Betrothal?: Scriptural Romance – Part 2 .np. http://www. boldchristianliving.com/articles/romance2.htm., August 10, 2001.

———. The Bold Parenting Seminar: Scriptural Strategies for Training Godly Sons and Daughters. np. nd. 6 cassettes.

———. The Dangers of Dating: Scriptural Romance – Part 1. np.http://www.boldchristianliving.com/articles/ romance1php, August 22, 2002.

———. Youthful Romance: Scriptural Patterns. np. http:// www.boldchristianliving.com/articles/tract.php. August 22, 2002.

MacArthur, John F. *Reckless Faith: When the Church Loses Its Will to Discern.* Wheaton: Crossway Books, Good News Publishers, 1994.

———. *John MacArthur's Bible Study: Guidelines for Singleness and Marriage*, I Corinthians 6:12-7:40. Panorama City, Calif.: Grace to You, 1975.4 cassettes.

MacArthur, John F., Jr. rev. ed. *Found: God's Will.* Colorado Springs: Chariot Victor Publishing, Cook Communications, 1977.

———. *The MacArthur New Testament Commentary:* I Corinthians. Chicago: Moody Press, 1984.

———. *The MacArthur New Testament Commentary: Matthew 1-7.* Chicago: Moody Press, 1985.

Mack, Wayne A. *A Homework Manual for Biblical Living.* Vol. 1, *Personal and Interpersonal Problems.* Phillipsburg, N.J.: P&R Publishing, 1979.

Maher, Bridget. "The Devastation of Divorce." In Focus no. 228. Family Research Council, (September 6, 2000).

———. "Living Together." In Focus no. 230. Family Research Council, (September 8, 2000).

———. "Marriage: Key to Happiness." In Focus no. 227. Family Research Council, (September 7, 2000)

———. "Record High = Record Low." Washington Watch, Vol. 12, no. 7. FamilyResearch Council, (May 2001): 6.

———. "Restoring Marriage: A Return to Commitment." Washington Watch,vol. 12, no. 8. Family Research Council, (June 2001): 1.

———. "The State of the Family." In Focus no. 229. Family Research Council, (September 5, 2000).

Malphurs, Aubrey. *Biblical Manhood and Womanhood.* Grand Rapids: Kregel Publications, 1996.

Markman, Howard, Scott Stanley, and Susan L. Blumberg. *Fighting for Your Marriage: Positive Steps for Preventing Divorce and Preserving a Lasting Love.* San Francisco: Jossey-Bass Publishers, 1994.

Mattox, William R. Jr. "Rebuilding a Marriage Culture: Why Capturing Young People's Imagination Is Key." *Family Policy* 10, no. 3. Family Research Council, (1997): 1-7.

McDonald, Cleveland, Ph.D. *Creating a Successful Christian Marriage.* Grand Rapids: Baker Book House, 1975.

Media Critic. "Report Linking Cohabitation and
    Divorce Criticized." np. http://www.newswatch.org/
    mediacritic/feb99/000210m1.htm. August 24, 2000.

Morris, Henry M. *The Genesis Record: A Scientific &
    Devotional Commentary on the Book of Beginnings.*
    Grand Rapids: Baker Book House, 1976.

Morrish, George, comp. *A Concordance of the
    Septuagint.* Grand Rapids: Zondervan Publishing
    House, 1976.

Moule, H. C. G., D.D. 2nd ed. *Ephesian Studies:
    Lessons in Faith and Walk.* Great Britain: Fleming H.
    Revell Company, nd.

Nelson, Tom. *Love Song: From Attraction to Faithfulness.*
    np., 1991. 6 cassettes.

Neuer, Werner. *Man & Woman: In Christian Perspective.*
    Translated by GordonJ. Wenham. Wheaton, Ill.:
    Crossway Books, Good News Publishers, 1991.

Olson, David H., John DeFrain, and Amy K. Olson.
    Building Relationships: Developing Skills for Life.
    Minneapolis: Life Innovations, Inc., 1999.

Orr, James. *The International Standard Bible
    Encyclopaedia*, Vol. 3. Grand Rapids: Wm. B.
    Eerdmans Publishing Co., 1956.

Orr, Susan. "The State of the Family." At the Podium no.
    80. Family Resource Council, (May 4, 2001).

Packer, J. I. *A Quest for Godliness: The Puritan Vision
    of the Christian Life.* Wheaton, Ill.: Crossway Books,
    Good News Publishers, 1990.

Peace, Martha. *The Excellent Wife.* Bemidji, Minn.: Focus Publishing, Inc., 1995.

Pearl, Michael, and Debi Pearl. "To Betroth or Not to Betroth? That Is the Question." No Greater Joy Newsletter, Vol. 7 no. 1, 2001.

Petty, James C. *Step By Step: Divine Guidance for Ordinary Christians.* Phillipsburg, N.J.: P&R Publishing, 1999.

Phillips, Bob. *How Can I Be Sure?* Eugene, Ore.: Harvest House Publishers, 1999.

Phillips, Richard D., and Sharon L. *Holding Hands, Holding Hearts: Recovering a Biblical View of Christian Dating.* Phillipsburg. NJ.: P&R Publishing, 2006.

Piper, John. *Desiring God, Meditations of a Christian Hedonist.* Sisters, OR: Multnomah Publishers, 1996.

———, and Wayne Grudem, eds. *Recovering Biblical Manhood & Womanhood: A Response to Evangelical Feminism.* Wheaton, Ill.: Crossway Books, Good News Publishers, 1991.

Popenoe, David. "The Top Ten Myths of Divorce." The National Marriage Project. np. Online: http://marriage. rutgers.edu/pubtoptenmyths.htm. October 16, 2001.

———. "Cohabitation, Marriage and Child Well Being, A Cross-National Perspective." Piscataway, N.J.: The National Marriage Project, 2008.

Powlison, David. "Your Looks: What the Voices Say and the Images Portray." *The Journal of Biblical Counseling* 15, no. 2 (1997): 39-43.

———, and John Yenchko. *Pre-Engagement, 5 Questions to Ask Yourselves.* Phillipsburg, NJ: P&R Publishing, 2000.

Ramm, Bernard. *Protestant Biblical Interpretation: A Textbook of Hermeneutics.* 3rd. rev. ed. Grand Rapids: Baker Book House, 1970.

Randolph, Paul. "The Family Covenant Model, Part 1: A Biblical Model of the Family." *The Journal of Biblical Counseling* 15, no. 2 (1997): 17-21.

Rienecker, Fritz. *A Linguistic Key to the Greek New Testament.* Translated by Cleon L. Rogers, Jr. Grand Rapids: Regency Reference Library, Zondervan Publishing House, 1976.

Risk, William P. *Dating & Waiting: Looking for Love in All the Right Places.* Grand Rapids: Kregel Publications, 2000.

Sande, Ken. 2nd ed. *The Peacemaker: A Biblical Guide to Resolving Personal Conflict.* Grand Rapids: Baker Books, 1997.

Scott, Stuart. *The Exemplary Husband: A Biblical Perspective.* Bemidji, Minn.: Focus Publishing, Inc., 2000.

Smith, Winston. "Wisdom in Relationships." *The Journal of Biblical Counseling* 19, no. 2 (2001) : 32-41.

Stanton, Glenn T. "Twice as Strong: Two Parents-One Healthy Child." np. http://www.family.org/cforum/research/papers/a0002969.html. July 6, 2001.

Street, John D. *Purifying the Heart of Sexual Idolatry.* Diss.,Westminster Theological Seminary, 2002.

The National Marriage Project. *The State of Our Unions 1999: The Social Health of Marriage in America.* Piscataway, N.J.: Rutgers, The State University of New Jersey, 1999.

——. *The State of Our Unions 2000: The Social Health of Marriage in America.* Piscataway, N.J.: Rutgers, The State University of New Jersey, 2000.

——. *The State of Our Unions 2001: The Social Health of Marriage in America.* Piscataway, N.J.: Rutgers, The State University of New Jersey, 2001.

Thompson, John W. God's Design for Scriptural Romance Part 1: Rediscovering the Timeless Truths. np., September 18, 2002. http://www.patriarch.com/courtshipjt1.html.

——. God's Design for Scriptural Romance Part 2: Dealing With the Dating Dilemma. np., September 18, 2002. http://www.patriarch. com/courtshipjt2html.

——. God's Design for Scriptural Romance Part 3: Preparing Your Children for Biblical Betrothal. np., September 18, 2002. http://www.patriarch.com/courtshipjt3.html.

——. God's Design for Scriptural Romance Part 4: Choosing a Spouse by Faith, Not Feelings. np, September 18, 2002. http://www.patriarch.com/courtshipjt4.html.

——. God's Design for Scriptural Romance Part 5: How to Marry – The Friendship Stage. np, September 18, 2002. http://www.patriarch.com/courtshipjt5.html.

———. God's Design for Scriptural Romance Part 6: How to Marry – The Courtship Stage. np, September 18, 2002. http://www.patriarch.com/courtshipjt6.html.

Tripp, Paul David. *Age of Opportunity: A Biblical Guide to Parenting Teens.* Phillipsburg, N.J.: P&R Publishing, 1997.

———. *Marriage: Whose Dream?* Phillipsburg, N.J.: P&R Publishing, 1999.

Tripp, Tedd. *Shepherding a Child's Heart.* Wapwallopen, Pa.: Shepherd Press, 1995.

Vantassel, Stephen. "Celibacy: The Forgotten Gift of the Holy Spirit." *The Journal of Biblical Counseling* 12, no. 3 (1994): 20-23.

Vincent, M. R. *Word Studies in the New Testament.* Mac Dill AFB, Florida: Mac Donald Publishing Company, nd.

Wagner, David M. "Divorce Reform: An Idea Whose Time Is Coming." *Family Policy.* 10, no. 5. Family Research Council (September 1997): 1-8.

Walvoord, John F and Roy B. Zuck. *The Bible Knowledge Commentary*, New Testament Edition. Wheaton, Ill.: Victor Books, 1983.

Warren, Neil Clark. *Finding the Love of Your Life.* Colorado Springs: Focus on the Family Publishing, 1992.

———. *Finding the Love of Your Life: The Road to Marriage From Start to Finish.* np., nd., cassettes.

———. *How to Know If Someone Is Worth Pursuing in Two Dates or Less.* Nashville: Thomas Nelson Publishers, 1999.

Welch, Edward T. "Self Control: The Battle Against 'One More'." *The Journal of Biblical Counseling* 19, no. 2. (2001): 24-31

———. *When People Are Big and God Is Small.* Phillipsburg, N.J.: P&R Publishing, 1997.

———. "Who Are We? Needs, Longings, and the Image of God in Man." *The Journal of Biblical Counseling* 13 no. 1 (1994): 25-38.

West, Jim, Pastor. *The Art of Choosing Your Love.* Palo Cedro, Calif.: Christian Worldview Ministries, 1994.

White, Genevieve M. *Daughters of Sarah.* Columbus, Ga.: Brentwood Christian Press, 1991.

Wigram, George V. and Ralph D. Winter. *The Word Study Concordance.* Wheaton, Ill.: Tyndale House Publishers, Inc., 1978.

Wilson, Douglas. *Her Hand in Marriage: Biblical Courtship in the Modern World.* Moscow, Idaho: Canon Press, 1997.

———. *Reforming Marriage.* Moscow, Ind.: Canon Press, 1995.

Wilson, P. B. *Knight in Shining Armor.* Eugene, Ore.: Harvest House Publishers, 1995.

Wilson, William. *New Wilson's Old Testament Word Studies.* Grand Rapids: Kregel Publications, 1987.

Wright, Norman H. rev. ed. *Premarital Counseling: A Guidebook for the Counselor.* Chicago: Moody Press, 1982.

Counseling One Another

This paradigm-shifting book helps believers understand the process of being transformed by God's grace and truth, and challenges them to be a part of the process of discipleship in the lives of their fellow brothers and sisters in Christ.

"This book gets it right! Comprehensive and convincing, *Counseling One Another* shows how true biblical counseling and preaching fit hand-in-glove. Those who preach, teach or counsel regularly are sure to benefit greatly from this helpful resource."
—**Dr. John MacArthur,** Pastor, Grace Community Church; President, The Master's College and Seminary

Christ-centered, comprehensive, compassionate and biblical. Christians would be wise to read and reread *Counseling One Another.*
—**Bob Kellemen,** Executive Director of The Biblical Counseling Coalition

Buy the paperback, get the ebook free!

Shepherd Press

shepherdpress.com

LifeLine
Mini-Books

Features of LifeLine Mini-Books:

• Written for ordinary readers as well as counselors and church ministers

• Includes personal application projects and Bible study suggestions

• Centered on the gospel

• Written by men and women with experience in helping others

More titles available and forthcoming

Help! Someone I Love has Cancer
Help! He's Struggling with Pornography
Help! My Toddler Rules the House
Help! I'm a Slave to Food
Help! My Teen Is Rebellious
Help! She's Struggling with Pornography
Help! I Feel Ashamed
Help! I Am Depressed
Help! I Can't Handle All These Trials
Help! I'm Living with Terminal Illness
Help! I Can't Forgive
Help! Someone I Love has Alzheimer's
Help! My Friend is Suicidal
Help! My Teen Struggles with
    Same-Sex Attraction
Help! Someone I Love has Been Abused
Help! I Can't Get Motivated
Help! My Anger is Out of Control
Help! I'm in a Conflict
Help! I'm Being Deployed
Help! I've Been Traumatized by Combat

"These little books are directly targeted to the issues that we all face and they hit the bulls-eye. They are faithful to Scripture and they demonstrate insight into its application. Churches need to make these available for their congregations."

—**John MacArthur,** Pastor, Grace Community Church; President, The Master's College and Seminary

"These mini-books are exactly the kind of books you'd want to have available to you at church—short, biblical and inexpensive enough to give away."

—**Tim Challies,** Blogger

An imprint of
Shepherd Press

shepherdpress.com/lifeline

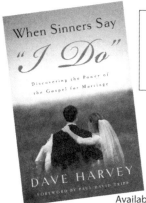

When Sinners Say "I Do" is also available with *The Study Guide*, as audio book and now with a full teaching **DVD** series.

Audio Book
Available as download at
shepherdpress.com

Available as
e-book also

Available on DVD or online streaming via Vimeo.

Marriage is the union of two people who arrive at the altar toting some surprisingly large luggage. Often it gets opened right there on the honeymoon, sometimes it waits for the week after. The Bible calls it sin, and understanding its influence can make all the difference for a man and a woman who are building a life together.

In this eight-session video series, Dave Harvey engages his audience with humor and honesty as he speaks about sin and the power of the gospel to overcome it. He opens the delightful truth of God's word and encourages his audience to see more clearly the glorious picture of what God does when sinners say "I do."

Watch Dave Harvey's introduction to the series online.

www.shepherdpress.com

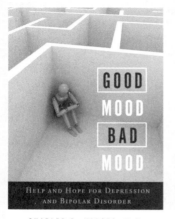

CHARLES D. HODGES, M.D.

Depression and bipolar disorder are two of the most common diagnoses made in medicine today. Are we in an epidemic of bad moods or is there another explanation? *Good Mood, Bad Mood* examines whether it is an epidemic or if we have simply changed how we label depression. While medical treatment is now the commonly accepted way to deal with pain and sadness, its promise has not been fulfilled. Dr. Charles Hodges offers an explanation to help the reader see the importance of sadness and the help and hope that God gives us in his Word.

Charles D. Hodges Jr., M.D. is a family physician who practices medicine in Indianapolis. He is a graduate of the Indiana University School of Medicine, board certified in Family medicine and Geriatrics and is a licensed marital family therapist.

Web Special:
Buy the paperback at
ShepherdPress.com, get
the ebook free!

"Dr. Hodges has given the church an important resource in *Good Mood, Bad Mood.* With the scientific acumen of a physician and the loving concern of a brother in Christ, Dr. Hodges cuts through the morass of solutions for sadness, depression, mania or bipolar disorders. Written for the layperson but detailed enough for the physician or counselor, this book is for anyone who struggles with troubling moods and for those who help them."
—**Elyse Fitzpatrick,** Author, speaker and counselor

Shepherd Press

shepherdpress.com